MRS. GROSSMAN'S
CREATIVE STICKER ART
for SCRAPBOOKS

200 simple yet sensational sticker ideas

Andrew goes
fishing with
his uncle Randy
and his cousins
Caleb and Josh.

Bass Lake,
Utah 2002.

CATCH
OF THE DAY

M
MEMORY
MAKERS
BOOKS

MRS. GROSSMAN'S PAPER COMPANY

Founder & President Andrea Grossman

Art Direction Sherryl Kumli, Gigi Sproul

Art Designers Kelly Carolla, Andrea Grossman, Andrea Joy Johnson, Tami Lovett, Amy Jill Wallace, Barb Wendel

Art Assistance Shannon McMath Aja, Raul Chacon

Copywriter Tracey Trumbo

Special thanks also to Sue Ferguson, Sandi Genovese, Leslie Randle and Linda Risbrudt

MEMORY MAKERS BOOKS

Executive Editor Kerry Arquette   Founder Michele Gerbrandt

Senior Editor MaryJo Regier

Art Director Andrea Zocchi

Designers Nick Nyffeler, Jennifer Pollman

Craft Editor Jodi Amidei

Art Acquisitions Editor Janetta Abucejo Wieneke

Photographer Ken Trujillo

Contributing Photographers Brenda Martinez, Terry Ownby, Ruth Ann Praska, Jennifer Reeves

Contributing Writer MaryJo Regier

Editorial Support Karen Cain, Emily Curry Hitchingham, Lydia Rueger, Dena Twinem

Memory Makers® Mrs. Grossman's Creative Sticker Art for Scrapbooks

Published by Memory Makers Books, an imprint of F+W Publications, Inc.

12365 Huron Street, Suite 500, Denver, CO 80234

Phone 1-800-254-9124

First edition. Printed in the United States.

08 07 06 05 04 5 4 3 2 1

Library of Congress Cataloging-in-Publication Data

Grossman, Andrea
     Mrs. Grossman's creative sticker art for scrapbooks : 200 simple yet sensational sticker
ideas.-- 1st ed.
        p. cm.
     Includes index.
     "Mrs. Grossman's Paper Company and Memory Makers Books join forces to bring you
innovative scrapbook page ideas featuring the stickers you love the most"--Cover.
     ISBN 1-892127-39-3
        1. Photographs--Conservation and restoration. 2. Photograph albums. 3. Scrapbooks. 4.
Stickers. I. Title: Creative sticker art for scrapbooks. II. Mrs. Grossman's Paper
Company. III. Memory Makers Books. IV. Title

TR465.G79 2004
745.593--dc22

                                                        2004049853

Distributed to trade and art markets by

F+W Publications, Inc.   4700 East Galbraith Road, Cincinnati, OH 45236   Phone 1-800-289-0963

ISBN 1-892127-39-3

In its 25th year, Mrs. Grossman's Paper Company enjoys over 200 daily visitors at their Petaluma, California, production facility, company store and sticker museum. For more information, call 1-800-429-4549. Visit us on the Internet at www.mrsgrossmans.com.

Memory Makers Books is the home of *Memory Makers*, the scrapbook magazine dedicated to educating and inspiring scrapbookers. To subscribe, or for more information, call 1-800-366-6465. Visit us on the Internet at www.memorymakersmagazine.com.

This book belongs to

_____

We dedicate this book to sticker lovers and scrapbook artists everywhere whom we
hope to inspire with these special ideas created just for you.

Table of Contents

2 Building With Stickers 40-69

3 Embellishing Stickers 70-99

Michele
&
Andrea

"True friends are
never apart,
maybe in distance,
but not in heart."
author unknown

Spring 2004

Introduction

Andrea In 1979, when we made our first sticker, and subsequently launched an industry, we had no idea where this was going. Kids madly collected stickers for the next six years and we had a wonderful time creating bright and colorful images that captured the attention of young and old alike. When the fad subsided and we were wondering what happened, we found ourselves linked with a large group of women who were using our stickers, of all things, in their family scrapbooks. What a perfect fit for our company that majored in family values and activities.

I can vividly remember the day I met Michele Gerbrandt. It was at a trade show and she shared with me her bold adventure: to publish a magazine called *Memory Makers* for the scrapbooking market. I admired her vision and her courage! I am eternally grateful that her dream was realized, because it has, among other good things, created a friendship that I treasure. I have some incredible memories of times shared with Michele and her family.

Scrapbooking with stickers has become a passion unlike anything I have seen in my 25 years in the industry and has kept us on our toes creating new images, new materials, new looks for the ever-increasing group of people who love their memories. What a blessing!

Michele From my first scrapbook page over 10 years ago until now, stickers have always been a favorite medium. They are fun to work with, easy to use and help me create great scrapbook pages. Early on I was exposed to Mrs. Grossman's stickers and quickly began collecting every design, style and size.

Little did I know then that I would one day get the opportunity to meet the real Mrs. Grossman and over the years develop a loving and caring friendship. It all started from a chance passing in an elevator at a trade show. Andrea and I began talking, which led to dinner and to future plans. We knew we had much to share.

As we worked together over the years, I grew to love Andrea not only as a mentor and a friend, but like family. I am excited that we are able to work with Mrs. Grossman's Paper Company to bring you innovative scrapbook page ideas using stickers you have already grown to love.

In this book, you will learn fun and creative ways to incorporate stickers into your scrapbook page designs. But more than that, you will never look at your sticker supply in the same way again. You will view your stickers in a whole new light—a light full of invigorating choices and endless possibilities!

Scrapbooking With Stickers

Before templates, colorants and embellishments, scrapbooking was an art of storytelling using photographs and plain white paper. As this art form re-emerged in the late 1980s, stickers became popular in albums because they helped make these stories more interesting. And today, they still do.

Stickers represent icons that everyone can identify with. They make people smile! They add color, beauty and an element of fun. Fun to use and fun to look at, stickers don't require a lot of artistic endeavor or time. As your love for this purposeful craft and the number of sticker choices continue to grow, you'll always find a sticker to help share your story.

Continuity is key. Continuity of colors, style and your story encourages readers to look at each and every page, building their excitement as they approach the end of your story. Continuity does not mean eliminating the element of surprise—a pop-up page, a bright splash of color or a pocket filled with postcards or journaling—to keep readers entertained.

Begin by spreading out select photos that you wish to scrapbook, then choose paper colors based on your photos. As a general rule, use lighter paper colors if your photos have dark backgrounds. Likewise, if your photos have light backgrounds, darker paper colors will help them stand out on the page. Select one paper color for the page background, drawing just one color from the photos. Then choose one to three additional paper colors whose colors also show in your photos and are complementary to your paper background.

With photos and papers determined, let the fun with sticker selection begin! Start by selecting stickers that represent your photo or page idea theme. But don't limit yourself there! Sometimes the best stickers to use have little to do with the obvious theme of your photos. Note below that bathroom, moving and travel-related stickers were selected to help tell the story shown in these photos of an adventurous cat. And now turn to page 29 to see how well the cat and these stickers work in unison with the photos to become "The World According to Bentley," a fun and unique scrapbook page with a hidden journaling panel that documents Bentley's feline frolicking.

Use this book to help you think of fresh new ways to tell your photo stories with stickers. By carefully choosing the stickers and artwork, using many of the techniques presented in this book, you can help your photographs communicate a story that is uniquely your own. Enjoy discovering the art of scrapbooking with stickers!

The Right Tools Make It Easy

A cutting mat, paper trimmer and scissors with long, pointy blades are necessities. A craft knife, metal straight-edge ruler and a pencil are also helpful. Don't be afraid to cut your stickers. It won't hurt them. Redesign a sticker by cutting leaves or stems off flowers. Trim a sticker to fit inside or on top of another sticker or scene. For a precise cut, trim the sticker while it is still on the liner paper.

Tweezers help you place tiny stickers and reposition or move stickers on your pages. Lightly placing stickers on the surface makes them easy to relocate. Once you're happy with the arrangement, press them down firmly using your fingertips or a burnishing tool.

Self-adhesive foam tape or foam spacers, a small brush and some baby powder or cornstarch can be used to pop stickers off your pages. Just place a small piece of foam tape on the back of a sticker, leaving the tape's liner in place. Lightly dust the back of the sticker with powder to neutralize the adhesive. Remove the liner and attach the sticker to your page or artwork.

Additional Tools & Supplies

Adhesive remover
Bone folder
Decorative scissors
Embossing stylus
Eyelet setter
Glue pen
Hammer
Journaling pen
Punches
Removable artist's tape
Sandpaper, fine-grain
Tape roller
Wax paper or excess sticker liner paper
Scrapbook colorants & embellishments

Sticker Troubleshooting

Use these helpful tips to get out of any sticky sticker situation:

Adding Dimension

1 Attach small pieces of double-stick foam mounting tape to the backside of each sticker, leaving the tape liner in place. Foam tape pieces should be small enough to not show from the front of the sticker art. You will probably not need more than a few pieces of foam tape per sticker.

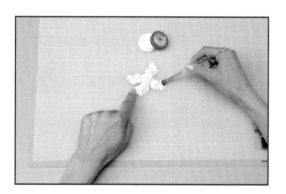

2 Lightly dust the back of the sticker with baby powder, talc, flour or cornstarch. You can use a small brush or cotton swab. This neutralizes the adhesive so that each sticker will stay lifted up off the art surface, even when the book or album is closed.

3 Gently remove tape liner and use the foam tape to attach sticker to your art surface.

Lining Up Letter Stickers

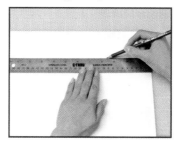 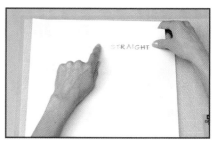

1 Determine where to place letters on the page. To place stickers in a straight line, mark this area using a pencil and a ruler.

2 Fold a piece of sticker liner paper, waxy side up, making a crease to use as a baseline. Place the bottom edge of each letter on a scrap of sticker liner paper. Position letters across paper on drawn line and carefully fold back the sticker liner, pressing the lower half of the letters down, then carefully pulling the sticker liner up holding the letters in position. Press letters firmly in place. Use a circle or shape template to draw lines for other letter position shapes.

Mitering Corners

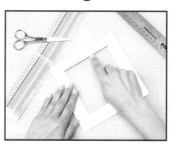 

1 Measure and place first Design Lines strip down, leaving a blunt straight edge on both ends.

2 Measure and cut a second Design Lines strip, cutting one end at a 45-degree angle.

3 Place the angled-cut end over the first Design Lines as shown creating a perfect "mitered" corner. Repeat with the third side and complete the fourth side with two more angled cuts.

Preventing Tangles or Tears

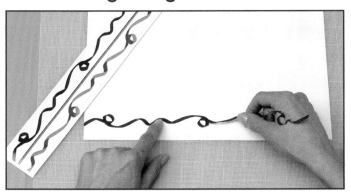

1 Help prevent long border stickers from tangling, tearing or sticking on unwanted areas by sticking one end to your hand while laying the other end down in place on the page.

Removing Wrinkles

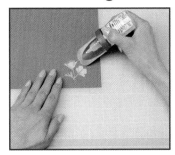 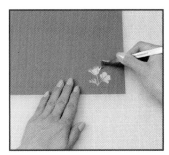

1 Use un-du adhesive remover to pry the sticker up, relieving the wrinkle. Once it dries, the back of the sticker will become tacky again, but more adhesive might be necessary.

2 Using tweezers, gently pull the wrinkle from the sticker and flatten with your finger, adhering properly in its place.

Fixing a Torn Sticker

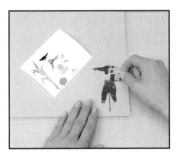 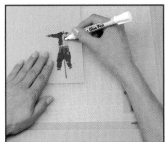

1 Overlap the ripped pieces slightly so the jagged edges do not show.

2 Coat the repaired sticker by using a clear adhesive over the seam to prevent ripped edges from peeling.

More Troubleshooting Tips

- Build your design on a piece of extra liner or wax paper. Tape a large piece of wax paper over album page and begin designing. When stickers are arranged as desired, transfer the stickers from the wax paper to the page.

- Not sure where a sticker will look best? Use tweezers to hold it over your artwork, allowing you to see what you're doing more easily. When you place a sticker on a page, position it lightly so it can be removed easily. To lift a sticker off the surface, slide a blank piece of liner paper, waxy side up, under the sticker's edge. Slowly "seesaw" the liner paper under the sticker until it is completely on the liner paper.

- Before placing stickers on a surface, look closely for "dams." These are the inner sticker bits that are too tiny for the production machinery to remove. A craft knife makes this a cinch.

- Change your mind and want to move a sticker? Use an adhesive remover such as un-du—a safe and reliable product available in craft and stationery stores.

- To prevent longer border stickers from ripping, leave them on the liner paper and carefully apply to page by peeling up small sections at a time.

- Remove stickers from liner paper carefully to prevent wrinkles. Peel them off slowly, from the bottom to the top, lifting upwards.

- When you're finished with the sticker art, place a piece of scratch paper over the surface of the art or album page and "burnish" the stickers down by rubbing the paper firmly with your hand or a smooth object like a bone folder.

- Organize stickers by color or theme to create a library, making it easy to find specific designs while you're working. Storage options include boxes with dividers, binders and notebooks with sleeves or an expandable file. Save bits and pieces separately to use for collage and single embellishments. Keep stickers in a safe, dry place to prevent curling and exposure to direct sunlight or moisture.

CHAPTER ONE
Basic Sticker Art

At first glance, you might not know what to do with a sticker. Don't be scared! It may be small. It's definitely sticky. But as a scrapbooker, you'll soon find that stickers can be your best friends. Available in all themes, shapes and sizes, stickers are basic design tools for every page you create. Simply stick one on the page and you're done!

Stickers can also be used for more than filling in those empty white spaces between your photos. As the first chapter begins, you'll gather ideas for how to use stickers as borders and frames for your pages and photos. You'll learn to create decorative corners, page edges and medallions. You'll find tips for making the task of journaling easy and fun! Whether it's combining stickers with letters for captivating titles, building elaborate sticker-art scenery or using a single design to create your own page background, you'll discover that stickers are an essential part of every page.

Hundreds of imaginative ideas and simple techniques await you!

Borders

Solid, patterned, or even textured Design Lines™ (DL) and sticker borders frame photos, journaling panels and page elements. Place borders directly on the page edge or ¼" to ½" from the edge to create an elegant margin. Mix, match and layer different border widths, patterns and colors to create a new border for each and every page. Imaginative active edges and graduated pages invite your reader to find out what awaits them at the next turn of a page.

Maui

SOFTEN STICKERS WITH A PEEK-A-BOO BORDER

Page edges, individual photos and panels are framed with bold purple Design Lines, adding contrast to the peek-a-boo stickers softened with a vellum overlay. Follow the steps below to create the background. Mount photos and journaling panel. Use a few of the remaining flower stickers to accent page title and photos, attaching with foam tape to add dimension. Try any theme stickers beneath vellum to create a contrasting border with visual interest.

Stickers Posh Tropical Flowers, Posh Parrots, Jewel Tone Slivers DL; **Paper** dark green and sage cardstocks, white vellum; **Other** alphabet die cuts (Sizzix)

How to Create a Peek-A-Boo Border

1 Cut a 10" square out of the center of the dark green cardstock leaving outside edges of 12 x 12" page intact to form a frame; set square aside for top of page. Trim vellum to 11" square.

2 Decorate outside edge of sage cardstock with tropical flower stickers, then trim ⅛" strips from outer edges of page, trimming any excess sticker overlap. Frame with purple Design Lines stickers.

3 Attach sticker-decorated sage cardstock on top of 12 x 12" green frame. Soften the sticker colors by placing the piece of vellum on top of the frame and then attach the 10" green cardstock square in the center.

Grand Canyon

SET THE STAGE WITH A SCENIC BORDER

A simple theme-related border across the upper or lower edge of the page helps set the stage for photos. Cut green hills from cardstock; top with train sticker. Place tiny people in front of train, attaching them to page with small pieces of foam tape. Construct journaling panel from parchment framed with strips of wood-grain paper. Use layers of scallop-edged tan cardstock for roof. Add journaling to complete page.

Stickers 440 Train DL, School, Fir Tree, Woodland Animals, Alphabitsy; **Paper** black, green and tan cardstocks, Mrs. Grossman's Sage Advice Ribbed cardstock, wood-grain paper (Golden Oak), cream-colored parchment; **Other** scallop decorative scissors

Picnic

MAKE A SCENIC BORDER TITLE

Frame outside edges of page with checkerboard sticker borders. Place a thin border inside wide border for contrast. Use narrow sticker borders to frame individual paper panels and photographs. Top letter stickers with smaller stickers or pieces cut from stickers to create a decorative title. Arrange your own sticker picnic on bright yellow paper to highlight the journaling panel.

Stickers Red Stickers By The Yard, Yellow Vellum Alphabet, Insects, Picnic, Groceries, Fruit, Primary Slivers DL, Swimming Gear, Grass; **Paper** white cardstock; **Other** 1½" square paper punch

Time to Stop and Smell the Flowers

CROP AND LAYER GRADUATED PAGES

Layered borders and delicately decorated page edges draw your reader into the story, revealing a new element or surprise each time they turn a page. Look for sticker designs printed in "mirror image" to use for this technique. To create this layered look, identify the number of pages you'd like to include in this special album section. Follow the steps below to build the graduated pages. Layer accented pages atop bottom or final page and trim, if needed, to line up pages. Mat photos and journaling with pieces of deckle-edged vellum and frame with narrow border. Complete the album by adding journaling and floral sticker bouquets tucked inside vellum pockets.

Stickers Studio Line Wildflowers, Studio Line Butterflies, Vellum Deckle & Lines DL, Streamers DL, Ribbon DL, Twist & Torn DL, Rainbow DL, Soft Shade Sliver DL, White Alphabet, Classic Alphabet; **Paper** Mrs. Grossman's Plain Vanilla Ribbed cardstock; white, green and pink vellum; **Other** gold paint pen; paper trimmer

How to Crop Graduated Page Edges

1. Trim down the right margin of each album page in ¾", ½" and then ¼" increments, leaving the last page full-size.

2. Work from the last page forward, accent the right edge of each page with vellum Design Lines stickers.

3. Slightly bend butterfly wings up, then use small pieces of foam tape to adhere it and floral stickers back-to-back—aligning common edges with sticky sides together—along DL page borders in stair-stepped fashion to create decorative page tabs.

Quintana Roo, Mexico

BUILD A PROGRESSIVE FILMSTRIP BORDER

Create a clever filmstrip to showcase small sticker vignettes or actual photos. Punch black cardstock square with filmstrip punch to create single slide frame for top of page. Cut a 1⅜ x 11" strip of white cardstock to use at bottom of page. Layer narrow check border sticker between two solid black borders to create filmstrip effect on top and bottom edges. Punch twelve ¾" squares from blue vellum panels and create water scenes using small sections of Dolphins and Ocean stickers. Sequence dolphin's motions to give illusion he is swimming across strip. Splice small pieces of black border between each picture. Make 1½ x 1" dolphin scene to fit in slide frame at top of page. Finish with matted page title and journaling block.

Stickers Dolphins, Vellum Panels, Ocean DL, Basic Black & White DL; **Paper** Mrs. Grossman's Sage Advice Ribbed cardstock, black and white cardstocks; **Other** filmstrip punch (All Night Media)

Grandparents Day

CUT AND PASTE AN ALL-AROUND PAGE BORDER

Trim sides of yellow paper to create a scalloped edge. Show off your decorative edge by matting it with red cardstock. Adhere School Design Lines around edges to create border. Apply sticker letters onto School DL to create title. Place red color blocks on white paper and cut at diagonal to create quick page corners; mount with foam tape. Adhere additional school stickers on small squares; layer on page corners with foam tape. Layer black paper on wood-grain paper for chalkboard; embellish with additional stickers. Use a white pen to "chalk" the journaling.

Stickers Vellum Primary Color Blocks, School DL, Classroom Stuff, Casual Alphabet **Paper** red, yellow and black cardstocks; wood-grain paper (Golden Oak); **Other** white paint pen or marker

4th of July
COMPARTMENTALIZE WITH BUNTING BORDERS

Use decorative borders to organize or compartmentalize a page. Start by matting trimmed white cardstock with red cardstock. Center portrait on upper two-thirds of page; frame with Design Lines stickers. Top each journaling block with colorful swags, using foam tape beneath stickers to add dimension. Add additional DL stickers to lower edge of journaling blocks. Crop five photos vertically into 1¾ x 2¾" rectangles; mount and frame with DL stickers. Separate the smaller photos from the portrait with a bold blue border across the page.

Stickers Fourth of July DL, Bunting DL, Jewel Tone Slivers DL, Primary Slivers DL; **Paper** red and white cardstocks; **Other** foam tape

Santa Fe
COLOR BLOCK A GEOMETRIC TITLE BORDER

A simple geometric border adds spice to a page without stealing the show from photos. Begin by using the largest vellum blocks as background for your border. Add smaller squares in front, cutting a few in half diagonally to add patterns. Frame upper and lower edges of border with narrow black Design Lines. Use additional black borders and geometric shapes to add detail to title border and matted journaling panel. Accent photo mats with orange DL, round corners and adhere to page.

Stickers Warm Vellum Color Blocks, Cool Color Blocks, Concerto DL, Abigail Caps, Vellum Deckle & Lines DL; **Paper** cream and black cardstocks; **Other** corner rounder punch

Annie on the Farm

UNITE A SPREAD WITH SIDE BORDER VIGNETTES

Give a two-page spread a "pulled-together" look with custom-coordinated side borders. Begin by bordering outer page edges with strips of patterned paper and a contrasting Design Lines sticker. Borrow scenes and elements from your photos to build sticker art on small paper-punched squares or medallions. Use scissors to trim any undesired overlap on squares. Crop and mount photos. Finish with matted title and journaling block accented with green DL stickers and a tiny medallion taken from a photo.

Stickers Water DL, Green Hills DL, Horse, Barnyard, Cow, Horse Tack, Small Farm Animals, Primary Slivers DL, Primary DL **Paper** Mrs. Grossman's Buttered Corn Ribbed cardstock, yellow, orange polka dot (Paper Patch) and cream paper; **Other** square punch

Science Project

SHOWCASE A THEME WITH EDGE BORDERS

An underlying sticker edge border can reinforce any page theme. First, apply sticker sections around outer edges of page; trim off excess overlap. Accent a smaller sheet of cardstock with Design Lines stickers to mimic double matting; mount centered on page. Adhere large and circle-cropped photos, sticker title and journaling block; accent with additional blue DL and theme stickers. A silver paint pen can change letters from white to sterling.

Stickers Jewel Tone Slivers DL, Primary Slivers DL, Spider Webs, Science, White Alphabet, Silver Alphabitsy; **Paper** black, blue and white cardstocks; **Other** silver paint pen; circle cutter or jumbo circle punch

Mats & Frames

Remember, your pictures should be the stars of any scrapbook page. Use these simple matting and framing sticker techniques to showcase your photos while subtly reinforcing their theme.

Bath Time

DECORATE A HANDMADE FRAME

Soften a photo series with a delicate yet playful paper and sticker frame. Cut a frame from paper and decorate it with bubble stickers; trim away excess overlap around edges. Select a single photo or a cropped photo series and position on page, topping with frame. Trim frame edges with Design Lines or border stickers. Adhere vellum title at top of page. Add bathtub and journaling block at lower edge of page. Create "towel" by edging vellum with sticker border and folding to shape. Finish page with additional bubble stickers.

Stickers Vellum Bubbles, Aqua and Sky Vellum Alphabets, Blue Linen DL; **Paper** Mrs. Grossman's Twilight and Periwinkle Ribbed cardstock, white vellum; **Other** bathtub die cut or template (source unknown)

More Ideas

EXTEND A PHOTO MOSAIC SCENE Stickers Meadow DL

CREATE A CUSTOM FRAME Stickers Happy Birthday, Small Balloons, Primary Slivers DL

First Snow

ACCENT A LAYERED, COLOR-BLOCK PHOTO MAT

Layered mats of sticker-accented vellum and complementary-colored papers add striking contrast to a single photo. First, layer two shades of blue cardstock for background. Add vellum square and a vellum journaling block on background; trim with Design Lines and snowflake stickers. Layer vellum with color-blocked segments assembled opposite of the background blocks for contrast. Edge with additional DL stickers. Crop and mount photo; edge with DL stickers. Complete page with letter-sticker title and vellum journaling block.

Stickers Snowflakes, Soft Shades Sliver DL; **Paper** white vellum, light blue and heather blue paper (DMD)

Polar Bears

CREATE A STICKER WINDOW ILLUSION

Capture incredible photographs or expressions through picture "windows." Cut four 3¾ x 5¾" windows in the middle of a 12 x 12" page, leaving ⅛" margin around each picture. Attach a single layer of the page protector on the reverse side of the page to create the window "glass." Arrange photographs on second piece of paper. Mount window page on top, using small pieces of foam tape to attach pages. Border each window opening with a Design Lines. Layer and overlap alphabet letters with vellum water DL for title. Finish with journaling written directly on textile-patterned DL sticker.

Stickers Vellum Water DL, Gray Shade DL, Aqua Alphabet, Textile Pattern DL; **Paper** Mrs. Grossman's Glacier Blue Ribbed paper, second sheet of cardstock (any color); **Other** page protector or transparency

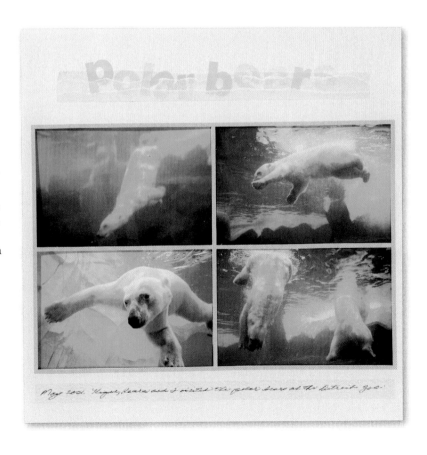

Corner Accents

Looking through grandparents' photo albums, you're likely to find a lot of those old black photo corners holding cherished pictures in place. Here are some colorful alternatives to the photo corners of old. Many of these corner ideas are also functional, so you can swap, replace or return original photos to the page at any time.

Skatin' Stu

ADD SIZZLE WITH STICKER PHOTO CORNERS

Dress up ready-made corners or create your own from narrow strips of cardstock. Begin by following the steps below to create photo corners. Insert corners of photos into handmade photo corners; mount on page. Embellish corners and title/journaling block with additional theme stickers mounted with foam tape for depth.

Stickers Primary Sliver DL, Skateboarders; **Paper** Mrs. Grossman's Atmosphere Ribbed cardstock, light green and white cardstocks; **Other** foam tape

How to Make Photo Corners

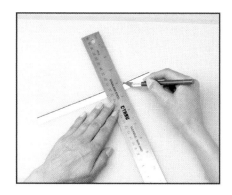

1 Cut strips of paper to ½" wide by 8" long. Decorate top edge of ½" wide paper strip with narrow Design Lines border. Cut each strip into 2" sections to create four photo corners.

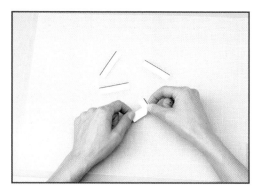

2 With borders facing down, fold down 1" section on left edge at a 45-degree angle.

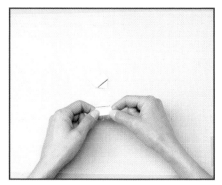

3 Fold remaining 1" section on right edge down, again creating a crease and 45-degree angle at top. Turn the paper to view triangular-shaped corner.

Karissa

ADD DIMENSION TO DECORATIVE CORNERS

Use foam tape to add dimension to your corners and page. Begin by positioning vellum medallion sticker on circle-cropped pieces of buff paper. Trim outside edge with scalloped scissors. Crop circle into quarters to make four corners. Mount corners on top of photos, using small pieces of foam tape to attach pieces to page. Repeat the corner accents on background and mat papers, accenting with Design Lines stickers. Complete page with letter sticker title and journaling block. Try this technique using patterned paper too!

Stickers Vellum Medallions, Textile Prints DL, Powder Alphabet; **Paper** citrine and buff papers (Paper Garden); **Other** foam tape; decorative scissors

At Play

LAYER CORNERS FOR PLAYFUL ELEMENT

Layering different Design Lines stickers is a quick-and-easy way to create fun little photo corners and mats for journaling blocks. Start by adhering two different DL borders at upper and lower edges of page. Cut each border sticker into four equal pieces and lightly dust the backs of the stickers with baby powder, talc or cornstarch to neutralize the adhesive. Fold the border over each corner of the photo and secure the ends directly to the album page. When photos are in place, the corners' powdery secret is hidden from sight. Add letter sticker title. Accent title with layered ladybug stickers mounted with foam tape; add pen stroke detail. Follow the tip below to create the journaling mat. Repeat the process to create mini medallions topped with additional ladybugs for the page.

Stickers Sheer Stripes Vellum DL, Ladybugs, Primary Slivers DL, Sky Alphabet; **Paper** white linen paper (Paper Patch); **Other** powder or cornstarch; foam tape

Up Close Create a plaid pattern by overlapping sections of striped vellum borders.

Backgrounds

We're all designers at heart! Create custom patterns and backdrops for your pictures by scattering stickers across the canvas of a blank scrapbook page. Repeat the same sticker image or design across the entire page, a solo panel or section to create a pretty pattern.

Gone Fishin'

CREATE A BACKDROP FOR A PHOTO FLIP BOOK

Sticker backgrounds can create a subtle yet sophisticated backdrop for a photo flip book mounted on a scrapbook page. Start with a blank scrapbook page and create an airy background using pieces of vellum stickers. Follow the steps below to make the photo flip book with progressive sticker-scene page edges. Mount single photo and flip book on page; frame page and pictures with Design Lines in contrasting colors.

Stickers Vellum Fall Leaves, Branches, Jewel Tone Slivers DL, Soft Shade Slivers DL, Fishing, Twist & Torn DL; **Paper** white and light green cardstocks; **Other** white adhesive tape

How to Create a Photo Flip Book

1 Cut two pieces of light green cardstock, cutting one at 5½ x 6" and the second at 9½ x 6". Fold the largest panel so the front is 4½ x 6" and back is 5 x 6". Fold the smaller panel so the front is 4 x 6" and a 1½ x 6" flap is at the back.

2 Decorate the front edges of each panel, layering photos, stickers and borders. Then frame and decorate the inside of each panel with stickers, title and journaling.

3 Assemble the flip book by placing the larger panel inside the smaller panel. Attach large panel to inside flap with glue, tape or adhesive.

It Was Love At First Sight

CREATE A GRIDLIKE BACKGROUND

Go behind the scene with a tone-on-tone "wallpaper" grid for an understated yet elegant background. Begin at the center of the page and work outward. Adhere whole or cropped stickers in grid-like fashion, overlapping corners of adjoining stickers and allowing rectangular glimpses of the background paper to show through. Mat title, photo and journaling on complementary-colored card-stock to complete the page.

Stickers Vellum Medallions in the same design; **Paper** Mrs. Grossman's Mauve-elous Ribbed cardstock, charcoal paper; **Other** square punches or scissors

Congratulations Graduate

LAYER A CELEBRATORY BACKGROUND

Choose colors from your photograph to create a fun and festive background. Layer and overlap vellum balloons at playful angles and streamers across a blank scrapbook page. Add the effect of motion by allowing balloons to overlap the edge of the page, trimming any excess overlap. Dance letter and number stickers across top and bottom edges of page for page title. Mount photo and finish with vellum-matted journaling block accented with Design Line stickers.

Stickers Spice and Celery Alphabets, Warm Numbers, Classic Alphabet, Congratulations, Vellum Streamers, Metallic Slivers DL, Vellum Balloons; **Paper** white cardstock, yellow vellum

A Valentine for Me?

SOFTEN BACKGROUND WITH VELLUM OVERLAY

Vellum overlays mute sticker colors, adding depth while bringing photos to the forefront of even the most decorated album page. Decorate the background page's side borders with stickers placed in an eye-pleasing pattern. Trim two vellum overlaps, cut to fit over side borders, with postage-stamp decorative scissors. Accent vellum overlaps with additional stickers. Crop and mount photos as desired; frame with Design Lines stickers. Add letter sticker title and finish with journaling on top of vellum in gold ink.

Stickers Love Stamps, Red Alphabet, Micro Hearts, Primary Slivers DL; **Paper** Mrs. Grossman's Grey Day Ribbed cardstock, white vellum; **Other** postage stamp scissors (Fiskars); gold paint pen

More Ideas

SOFTEN A CELEBRATORY TITLE
Stickers Vellum Alphabets, OP Confetti, Active Edge DL

CREATE A DIMENSIONAL SCENE
Stickers Game Birds, Brushstroke Grasses DL, Abigail Caps Alphabet

Titus at 6 Months

MUTE A MONOCHROMATIC STICKER MAT

Speak softly and warm the heart of a black-and-white photo with a muted, monochromatic mat. The depth provided by the sticker and vellum layers gives the illusion that the photo is behind a frame. Trim an 8½ x 11" sheet of ivory cardstock down to 8½ x 7". Use a pencil to lightly trace around a photo on ivory cardstock to create a 1½" frame around the photo. Fill the drawn frame outline with stickers, repeating design or pattern as desired. Trim off excess overlap from outer edges of cardstock. Cut vellum to size of cardstock; attach to cardstock, softening the sticker art. Top mat with photo accented with DL stickers. Layer vellum/sticker panel and photo atop background page trimmed with DL stickers. Finish with sticker-accented journaling block.

Stickers Brushstroke Branches, Metallic DL; **Paper** Mrs. Grossman's Just Plain Vanilla Ribbed cardstock, smooth ivory cardstock, Mrs. Grossman's Just Plain Vanilla vellum; **Other** gold pen

Baby Girl

SHADOW A REPETITIVE TITLE BACKGROUND

Vellum layered over a repetitious sticker pattern creates a shadow effect while mirroring the page title. Cut cream paper to a 10" square. Place same-design word stickers in diagonal rows across the paper; mount paper at center of a pink 12 x 12" background. Trim pink vellum to an 11" square; place over cream paper, securing each corner with a brad fastener. Position photo and page title on top, placing stickers directly on top of the twin images used to create pattern. Journal on the diagonal in silver ink to complete page.

Stickers PW Baby Girl, Soft Shade Sliver DL; **Paper** Mrs. Grossman's Strawberry Shake and Just Plain Vanilla Ribbed cardstock, Mrs. Grossman's Strawberry Shake vellum; **Other** silver brad fasteners; silver ink pen

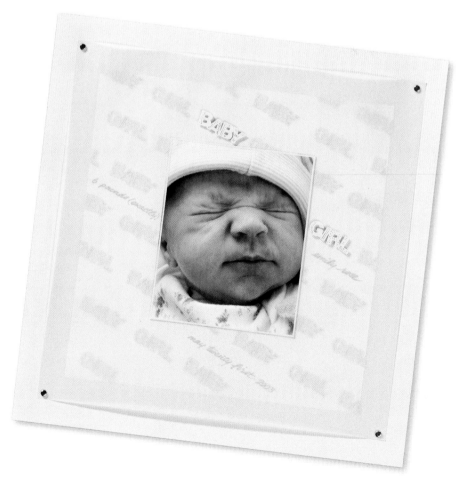

Medallions

Capture the story or theme of your page in a single square! Cut or punch squares of paper and decorate with sticker art scenes, from simple to sophisticated, to place at the top of your pages or highlight journaling panels. Frame medallions with narrow borders or mat with paper. Attach them to your page with a small piece of self-adhesive foam spacer to add dimension.

Florida

BUILD A DIMENSIONAL MEDALLION BORDER

Include the medallion theme on a page title and journaling panel for a designer look. First, mat photos with vellum edged with Design Lines stickers. Add a DL strip for page border. Punch or cut squares from cardstock; add DL edges. Build sticker scenes related to page theme. Use small pieces of self-adhesive foam spacers to "pop" stickers on square cardstock medallions. Don't be afraid to let stickers hang off the edge of the panels. This adds a sense of depth to your page. Simply powder the backs of the stickers to prevent them from sticking to the page. Assemble and adhere title medallion and journaling panel to complete page.

Stickers Florida, Hawaii, Vellum Sheer Stripes DL, Soft Shades Page Outline; **Paper** Blue Moon cardstock (Paper Garden), pale blue granite cardstock, pale pink vellum

More Ideas

ADD A BOLD TOUCH TO SOFT FLORAL MEDALLIONS

Stickers Jewel Tone Page Outline, Lavender

FRAME A COLORFUL, ARTISTIC SCENE

Stickers Vellum Color Blocks, Bear, Artist Gear

MAKE A LACY FLORAL MEDALLION

Stickers Lace Medallion, Rose Garden, Pastel Color Blocks, Soft Shade Slivers DL

CREATE A SOFT PAGE TITLE MEDALLION

Stickers Baby Boy, Vellum Panels, Blue Linen Ribbon DL

BUILD A FESTIVE CIRCUS SCENE ON THREE MEDALLIONS

Stickers Circus, Active Edge DL, Primary Slivers DL

New Puppy Ruby

LAYER STICKERS WITH DIE CUTS FOR MEDALLION SCENES

Layer medallions or panels of paper with die cuts and stickers to create stories and scenes for your page. Begin with cardstock borders across upper and lower edges of page. Mount photos edged with Design Lines stickers. Build matted, scenic sticker medallions related to page theme, using small pieces of self-adhesive foam spacers between layers to add depth. Complete page with letter stickers for title, bone stickers, and matted journaling.

Stickers Neighborhood Dogs, Giant Puppies, Custom Cars, Casual Alphabet, Grass, Circus, Soft Shade Slivers DL; **Paper** Mrs. Grossman's Periwinkle and Twilight Ribbed cardstocks, red cardstock, dark blue cardstock (DMD), wood-grain paper (Golden Oak); **Other** die-cut wagon (Sizzix)

The World According to Bentley

RECONSTRUCT AN ADVENTURE WITH SCENIC MEDALLIONS

Create the scenes or adventures from your pictures using stickers on small panels or medallions of paper. Adhere sticker scenes, alternating with medallion sticker scenes, across the bottom of your page. Mount three photos on page. Mount the fourth photo on a folded piece of cardstock the same size as photo for a hidden journaling panel. Frame photos with Design Lines stickers. Add letter sticker title and finish with journaling.

Stickers Basket, Giant Cats, Cat, Kittens, Bathtub, Baby's Toys, Moving Day, Luggage, Jewel Tone Slivers DL, Jewel Tone DL, Casual Alphabet, Alphabitsy; **Paper** Lambs' Wool paper (DMD), blue vellum; **Other** self-adhesive foam spacers

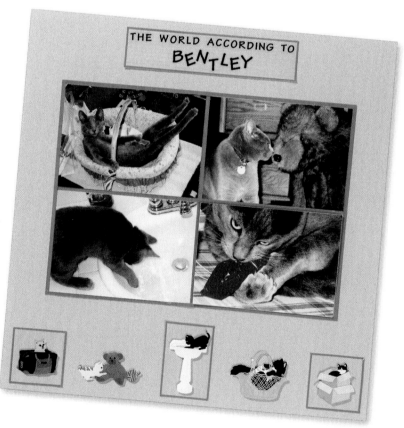

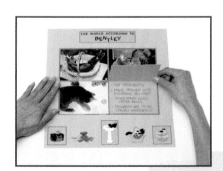

Up Close A folded paper panel holds the photo on front and journaling inside.

Storytelling

Every scrapbook page has a story to share! Here are some easy ways to illustrate your stories using children's colorful illustrations and elaborate sticker scenes. Creative cutouts, curious pockets and clever cards offer interactive ways to tell your story. You'll have so much fun that the stress of what to write on each and every page will simply disappear.

Self-Portrait

HIDE A STORY IN A JOURNALING POCKET

Move some of your children's favorite artwork from the refrigerator to the scrapbook with the help of a color copier and use a pocket to hold the secret story behind the artist's self-portrait. Begin with a color-block cardstock background. Photocopy and adhere artwork, sizing to fit page; edge with Design Lines stickers. Mount and edge photo in the same manner. Follow the steps below to create the sticker-scene pocket and hidden journaling panel. Make a matching title with additional letter and theme stickers.

Stickers Primary Slivers DL, Ext. Kids, Artist Gear, Beach, Casual Alphabet; **Paper** green, purple, lavender and white cardstocks; **Other** pattern on page 108; self-adhesive foam spacers

How to Build a Storytelling Pocket

1 Create a sticker scene related to the story of your scrapbook page on a piece of vellum edged with Design Lines stickers and matted with cardstock. Use self-adhesive foam spacers to pop up parts of the picture.

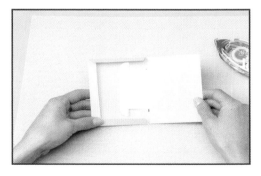

2 Photocopy and size the pattern on page 108 to fit sticker scene; transfer the pattern to colored cardstock and cut out. Score pocket on fold lines, cut the slot for an opening for the story panel and make the folds.

3 Insert the story panel through the slit leaving the wider ends in the pocket; make the folds and secure with permanent adhesive.

4 Glue the sticker scene to the front of the pocket. Mount pocket tabs onto page with the slot facing the direction from which you will pull the story panel.

The Beautiful Cotswolds
CUT A WINDOW FROM BACKGROUND FOR STORYTELLING SCENE

Narrate the story behind your photos with a window cutout to fill with journaling. Or let your vacation photo inspire the artwork by building a sticker scene to mount behind the window. Photocopy and size the pattern on page 109. Transfer pattern to background paper and cut out window. Build your sticker scene on a vellum "canvas," using smaller stickers in the background and larger stickers in the foreground to create the illusion of depth. Mount photos and edge with Design Lines stickers. Add letter stickers for title and journaling.

Stickers Twilight Alphabet, Classic Alphabet, Oak Tree, Park, Christmas Hearth; **Paper** Blue Moon (Paper Garden), white, brown and black cardstocks and blue and green vellums; **Other** pattern on page 109

Kegan's Chickens
USE STICKERS TO HELP TELL HIDDEN STORY

A sticker medallion reinforces the hidden story tucked behind a child's artwork. Begin with a cardstock border along lower page edge. Mount photo; edge with Design Lines stickers. Photocopy and size child's drawings; accent edges with DL stickers. Cut a card with a "lift tab" from cardstock the same size as artwork; mount drawing on front of card and journaling panel on inside; edge with additional DL stickers. Finish with letter sticker title and chicken-pen sticker scene.

Stickers Small Farm Animals, Jewel Tone Sliver DL, Metallic Sliver DL; **Paper** mustard, white, green and red cardstocks

Up Close Write your story on a panel or card and then cover it with paper matching the page background. Mount child's artwork on front and journaling on the inside. Attach panel to the page.

Title Pages

Introduce impact at the front of your album or in a special section by creating a personalized title page. Include a dedication if you're creating the album as a gift. Your date and signature will make your album even more meaningful to children and grandchildren. One spectacular photo and a title accented with stickers are all you need to set the stage for what's to come!

Our Trip to Yellowstone

USE STICKER SCENERY ON A TITLE PAGE

Placing stickers in letter-sticker title helps reinforce the theme of an album. Mat and mount photo. Cut small sections of stickers and place inside letter stickers. Tuck animals in the curves and spaces between words or letters. Duplicate elements of the scenery borrowed from the photo or title at the bottom of the page to complete your story, using self-adhesive foam spacers for depth.

Stickers Fir Tree, Classic Alphabet, Woodland Animals, Sky Alphabet; **Paper** Mrs. Grossman's Sage Advice and Twilight Ribbed cardstocks

More Ideas

CREATE A SPECIAL CITY NAME FOR A TITLE PAGE

Stickers Cityscape DL, Yellow Vellum Alphabet

COMMEMORATE AN EVENTFUL TRADITION WITH STICKERS

Stickers Fireworks, Sky Vellum Alphabet & Numbers

CAPTURE THE ESSENCE OF A SPECIAL PLACE IN A TITLE

Stickers Sea Creatures, OP Coral, Vellum Water DL, Aqua Vellum Alphabet

My Winter Vacation

JUMP-START A VACATION ALBUM WITH A CHILLY TITLE PAGE

Use a photo to tell the whole story. Complement it with a simple title of letter stickers accented with layers of icicle stickers. Construct ski accessories out of metallic stickers or paper. Mount additional icicles, layered with self-adhesive foam spacers for dimension, at the top of the page. Add number stickers for year to complete title page.

Stickers Icicles DL, Metallic Slivers DL, Ruby Stickers By the Yard, Twilight Alphabet, Classic Alphabet; **Paper** silver cardstock; **Other** self-adhesive foam spacers or foam tape

Our Special Day

LAUNCH THEME ALBUM WITH AN ELEGANT TITLE PAGE

Frame a page title in opulence with Design Lines borders. First, attach with pieces of foam tape to add several layers of dimension. Then, center periwinkle paper panels on page, adding a layer of vellum. Build frame from Greco Columns stickers, accenting with flowers and accessories. Finish by carefully positioning title on panel. It may help to arrange letter stickers on edge of sticker liner or ruler to make sure spacing is correct. Gently transfer to page, pressing letters down firmly.

Stickers Wedding Accessories, Greco Columns DL, Silver Deco Lace DL, Classic Alphabet; **Paper** Mrs. Grossman's Just Plain Vanilla and Periwinkle Ribbed cardstocks, white vellum

Our Christmas Album

CREATE A FESTIVE OPENING FOR CHRISTMASES PAST

Accent dramatic paper colors with simple sticker art. Include a photo inside the title panel to start your story on the title page, if desired. A bow on the edge of the panel will invite readers to look inside.

Stickers Christmas Garland DL, Metallic Slivers DL, White Alphabet, Christmas Greens; **Paper** chili and evergreen cardstocks; **Other** gold thread; ribbon bow

Page Titles

Creative sticker page titles help capture the essence of an entire page with just a word or two. Dress up basic block letters by entwining them with flowers, frills or maybe a frog. Accent vertical or horizontal sections of each letter with a small pattern or texture cut from stickers. Or, if you dare, replace an entire letter with a similarly shaped sticker!

Sisters

CREATE A PAGE TITLE WITH ELEMENTS FROM PHOTOS

Pulling inspiration from your photos is the easiest way to design a custom-coordinated page title. Mat and mount photos. Follow the steps below to layer stickers and letter stickers together, placing larger stickers in front and smaller stickers in back to create depth for a title and medallion; mat with cardstock. Add a journaling block to complete the page.

Photos: Val Westover

Stickers Poppy, Black-Eyed Susan, Meadow DL, Yellow Alphabet, Jewel Tone Sliver DL; **Paper** goldenrod and brown cardstocks

How to Add Dimension to a Page Title

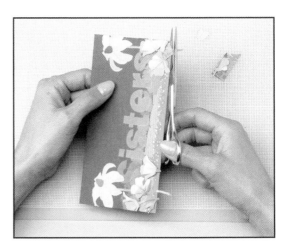

1 Place the Meadow Design Lines on a piece of extra liner paper. Spell "Sisters" across the top of the border. Add the Black-Eyed Susan stickers.

2 Create the next level of dimension by placing small pieces of foam tape on the backs of the Poppy stickers. Add a double layer or thickness of tape to two or three blooms. Lightly dust the backs of the stickers with powder. Place the Poppy greenery first, then the individual blooms.

3 Once the sticker title is complete, transfer it to a piece of brown cardstock. Carefully trim excess stickers from each edge. Attach panel to your page.

Frogs and Snails

INCORPORATE AN OLD SAYING INTO TITLE

Use stickers to spell out a saying that accentuates photos. Begin with a color-block background. Colorblock and mat photos in reverse colors and mount on page. Create matted title panels with large vellum letter and theme stickers. Add Casual Alphabet letters to further explain each title panel and add hand-lettering. Complete journaling panel with additional hand-lettering.

Stickers OP Tree Frogs, OP Bugs, Gt. Dogs, Puppies, Celery and Sky Alphabets, Casual Alphabet; **Paper** blue, white and apple green cardstocks

Uncle Frog

ADD PLAYFULNESS TO PAGE TITLE

Leaping frog stickers "hop" through the title on this page filled with pictures. A clever title can even bridge the gap when there's limited room for journaling on a page. Cut eight evenly spaced 3½" square "windows" in background paper; edge with Design Lines stickers. Mount seven photos behind background paper, centering each photo in a window and cropping if needed to fit. Create page title for eighth window with letter and frog stickers. Add journaling panels with self-adhesive foam spacers and additional frog stickers.

Stickers Celery Alphabet, Frogs, Primary Sliver DL; **Paper** Mrs. Grossman's Buttered Corn and Sage Advice Ribbed and white cardstocks

Up Close Frog stickers were placed beneath the vellum letters to give the title a sense of depth. Build your title on a piece of extra liner paper before moving it to your page.

Journaling With Stickers

Stickers do more than decorate. They help communicate! Use stickers to communicate emotions, places, things or even sounds in your journaling. You're likely to find everything you need in that box or drawer of sticker scraps. From dropped initials to rebus stories, you'll discover it's easy to say it with stickers.

Joe's Senior Football Season

USE STICKERS TO DEFINE JOURNALING

Use a computer to share narrative stories or family histories, then draw attention to the journaling's focus with vellum letter stickers. To offset extensive journaling, keep page layouts and artwork simple with fold-out photo panels that conceal more photo highlights inside. Cut two 4 x 12" cardstock photo panels from white cardstock; score at 6" and make the folds to create cards. Mount photo panels on page as shown; adhere photos, letter sticker title and flag sticker. Mat large photo and journaling block; adhere. Add vellum letter stickers over journaling. Coat sports-related stickers with black ink to create silhouettes; mount atop metallic background stickers and adhere along lower border of page.

Stickers Casual Alphabet, Football Gear, Spice and Celery Vellum Alphabets, Scrap Metal Blocks; **Paper** green, black, gold and white cardstocks; **Other** India ink or black inkpad

More Ideas

EDGE JOURNALING PANELS FOR SWEET SIMPLICITY

Stickers Lace Edging DL, Rosebuds

USE STICKERS TO ACCENT AND TACK DOWN JOURNALING

Stickers Vellum Violets, Cool Color Blocks

ACCENT PAGES TORN FROM TRAVEL JOURNAL

Stickers Vellum and Classic Alphabets, Rome

School's Out

ALLOW STICKERS TO HELP TELL THE STORY

Rebus journaling allows you to use stickers to represent an entire word. Invite your children to help! First, write your journaling on a scratch piece of paper and identify words that can be represented by a sticker. If you can't find the exact sticker match, combine numbers or letters to create a part or sound and complete the word. Accent page edges with Design Lines stickers. Create rebus journaling on complementary-colored vellum. Use the same concept to create a page title; mat and mount on page. Add matted photo to finish page.

Stickers Swimmers, Teen Tech, Soccer, Fruit, Puppies, Classroom Stuff, School, Fir Tree, Vellum Numbers, Vacation, Twist & Torn DL, Primary DL; **Paper** white and red cardstocks, yellow vellum

San Diego Zoo

FOCUS ON PHOTO THEME WHEN SELECTING STICKERS

Let the theme of your photos dictate your selection of stickers for rebus journaling. While stickers are still on the liner paper, try mapping out your story on a piece of scratch paper. Once you have the position and spacing finalized, write the story on the album page. The stickers are the last things you'll put on the page. Trim page, accent edges with Design Lines stickers and mount on background. Add letter sticker title, cropped and matted photo and journaling to complete page.

Rebus journaling by Jordan Dean, age 12

Stickers Alphabets, Numbers, Noah's Ark, Luggage, Vacation, Train, Chimpanzees, Tigers, Lion, Crocodile, Carnival Food, Elephant, Camel, Bugs, Birds, Glow Eyes, Metallic Sliver DL; **Paper** white and forest green cardstocks

Hidden Journaling Panels

"Who," "what," "where" and "when" are important elements on any page. And the answers to those questions become even more meaningful when they're written in your own hand or that of a close friend or relative. But journaling doesn't have to be limited to words on paper. Look what a few stickers and a little ingenuity can do! Turn your story into an interactive experience by using one of many hidden-panel techniques.

Party

CONCEAL JOURNALING IN A PRESENT

Wrap up your story using a piece of cream paper and ribbon-like stickers and bow. First, accent page edges with Design Lines sticker border. Accent photo edges with additional DL stickers, mat and mount on page. Adhere present sticker on a punched square of cardstock with self-adhesive foam spacer. For hidden journaling panel, fold rectangular cardstock panel in half so that one half is ¾" longer than the other. Fold the ¾" edge down to create the flap to hold panel closed. Trim flap edge with decorative scissors. Add DL stickers and sticker bow, dusting lower bow edges on the back to neutralize the adhesive backing. To make "hidden" journaling accessible, cut or slit the page protector and bring front panel and flap through. Readers can now view the whole story while your pages remain protected from smudges and fingerprints.

Stickers Bows, Gifts, Vellum Sheer Stripes DL, Soft Shade DL, Soft Shade Sliver DL, Sky and Lilac Alphabets; **Paper** Mrs. Grossman's Periwinkle and Lavender Sachet Ribbed cardstocks, cream paper; **Other** decorative scissors

More Ideas

CREATE SCENE WITH STICKERS AND JOURNALING

Stickers Bamboo DL, Vellum Water DL, Vacation

FRAME A PLAYFUL JOURNALING PANEL

Stickers Glitter Beads

GIVE A JOURNALING PANEL A SIMPLE CORNER EMBELLISHMENT

Stickers Vellum Vases, Spring Stems

Cows on Parade

HIDE AWAY JOURNALING WITH PHOTOS

Disguise the journaling panel at the top of your page by building a foldout panel that opens from the center of page with a tab lift. Trim a sheet of 12 x 12" cardstock to 11½" square. Use a metal straightedge ruler and bone folder to score a line 3⅞" from one edge of 11½" cardstock square. Make a fold on the line to create hidden panel and mount on page. Trim seven photo edges with Design Lines stickers around outer edges; mount photos on interior and exterior of foldout panel. Trim the remaining white space on the panel's interior with DL stickers and add journaling. Create a matted title with letter stickers. Make custom-coordinated sticker medallions by combining various parts of different stickers and adhere. Finish with a sticker "tab" on front of hidden journaling panel.

Stickers Cow, Sapphire Alphabet, Jewel Tone Page Outline, New York, Trick or Treaters, Giant Vehicles; **Paper** Mrs. Grossman's Twilight Ribbed cardstock, white cardstock

Celebrate With Bears

TUCK JOURNALING BEHIND A SHADOW BOX

Use a bookshelf filled with bears to share your "beary" special story. Begin by accenting page edges and photos with Design Lines stickers. Fold cream cardstock to create journaling panel. Write story inside. Decorate front with a bookshelf built from red paper. Use darker red paper for the top and inside shelves to create a sense of depth. Attach bookshelf to front of panel with self-adhesive foam spacers for lift. Fill shelves with sticker "toys," using additional foam spacers to create dimension. Create coordinating title with letter and bear stickers. Add photos to complete page.

Stickers Red Alphabet, Casual Alphabet, Blue Stickers By the Yard, Bear, Sm. Bears, Artist Gear, Beach, Christmas Hearth, Trim-a-Tree, Primary Sliver DL; **Paper** Mrs. Grossman's Just Plain Vanilla Ribbed cardstock, smooth ivory cardstock, two shades of red cardstock

CHAPTER TWO
Building With Stickers

Now that you've mastered the basics of using stickers in your scrapbook, it's time to have even more fun! Discover simple ways to bring motion, dimension and collage to your scrapbook stories. Add interaction with sticker pop-up pages, shaker boxes and shadow boxes. Create optical illusions, moving parts, panels and pockets. Combine stickers with paper to add woven patterns, playful plaids or whimsical wreaths to a spread.

You'll borrow from classic paper-crafting techniques and supplies easily found in your toolbox. Stretch your imagination by exploring new ways to use self-adhesive foam spacers or tape, scissors, punches, baby powder, vellum, tiny glass marbles, brad fasteners, color copies and more! Step-by-step instructions, patterns and templates make each technique easy to learn.

Your scrapbooks will soon be the talk of the town when your friends and family see what a few stickers and a little creative "know-how" can do! Building with stickers may be just the beginning once your imagination takes over.

Sticker Wreaths

Colorful leaf and floral wreaths adorn tables and doors in your home. We've taken three perennial favorites—fall leaves, children and white flowers—to show you what circles and stickers can do for a blank page or small photo. Start with the outline of a circular shape and carefully layer an assortment of sticker "foliage." Adding small pieces of self-adhesive spacers between the stickers builds fullness and dimension.

Make Your Life a Mission

CREATE A CIRCLE OF FRIENDS

People stickers, joined hand-in-hand, create a circle of unity for a mission, family reunion, classroom or any group-related scrapbook page. Mat photos and mount at four corners. Follow the steps below to create the wreath. Finish page with letter sticker title and matted journaling block.

Stickers Children DL, Casual Alphabet, Alphabitsy; **Paper** white and red cardstocks; **Other** pencil; protractor or dessert plate; craft knife

How to Build a Sticker Wreath

1 Use a pencil and compass or a dessert plate to lightly trace a large circle in the middle of your matted album page.

2 Use a craft knife to gently cut the children stickers apart, separating each sticker at the hands. Cover the drawn circle with stickers, layering children together into curved sections while tucking cut sections behind the neighboring sticker. You can do this step while stickers are still on the liner paper if you wish.

3 Transfer your artwork to the page. If a sticker "bumps" into a photo, either tuck the sticker's edge beneath the photo mat or carefully cut it and line up the cut edge of the sticker with the edge of the photo mat.

May 2003

ARRANGE AN ELEGANT FLORAL WREATH

Borrow flowers from the bride's bouquet or best dog to build a classic floral wreath. Accent background paper edges with Design Lines stickers. Mat photos with vellum and mount on page. Build the wreath on a piece of sticker liner. Start by tracing a circle on the liner paper. Using the same sprig of hydrangea blossoms, build the arrangement in a circular fashion, layering stickers on top of each other. Use small pieces of self-adhesive foam spacers on the backs of stickers that are at the front of the arrangement for depth and to make the wreath appear realistic. Add faux crystal accents and tuck loops of ribbon into the bottom of the wreath. Complete page with letter sticker title and vellum journaling block accented with DL stickers.

Stickers Rosebuds, Vellum Textile Prints DL, Soft Shade Slivers DL, Classic Alphabet; **Paper** peach cardstock, yellow vellum; **Other** compass or circle template; Mrs. Grossman's Opal Crystal Accents; 1/8" wide yellow ribbon

Fall

ASSEMBLE A CRISP AUTUMN WREATH

Frame a photo with a fabulous fall wreath with lifelike vellum leaves. Trim cream cardstock to 8" wide. Use a pencil and compass or graduated templates to lightly draw two concentric circles—one for the photo and one for the wreath. Carefully cut out the inner circle; mount photo behind the circle, securing photo in place on the back of the cardstock. Fold each leaf sticker in half lengthwise before placing on circular frame. Use powder to prevent leaves from sticking as shown below. Continue adding and powdering leaves until wreath is full. The finished wreath will have a ruffled effect on the inner and outer edges. Mount cream cardstock at center of tan cardstock background. Accent page and border edges with Design Lines stickers. Use additional DL stickers for journaling block, accented with more leaf stickers and a matted letter sticker title.

Stickers Vellum Fall Leaves, Earth Tone Page Outlines, White Alphabet, Ivy DL; **Paper** tan and cream cardstocks; **Other** protractor or circle template; baby powder, cornstarch or flour; small paintbrush

Up Close Use a small paintbrush to powder outer edges (not the center) of the leaf stickers to prevent leaves from sticking to the cardstock, the photo or each other.

Design Lines Scenes
Let us show you how to stretch your stickers!

Turn one sticker into six or more page elements by cutting scenic Design Lines stickers and landscape sticker borders into smaller sections. Center each section on a medallion panel to spread the story across an entire page. Layer patterned, playful or abstract borders on top of one another to create a decorative stack of paper panels for hundreds of imaginative uses.

Bodie, CA

REPRODUCE SCENIC PHOTO ELEMENTS

Pull design inspiration from your photos by re-creating the scenes in the photos with theme Design Lines stickers. Mat photos with vellum and mount on page. Cut the Western Town DL into smaller sections to create medallions and accent journaling panels. For an interesting visual, cut top edge of panel to follow the line of the rooftops. Complete page with vellum letter sticker title accented with a scenic medallion.

Stickers Spice Alphabet, Western Town DL, Warm Color Blocks; **Paper** cream and sand cardstocks, orange vellum; **Other** scissors

More Ideas

DESERT SCENE

Using two identical Desert Design Lines, cut and "pop" specific areas by placing pieces of one DL on top of corresponding DL using self-adhesive foam spacers.

NEW ENGLAND VILLAGE SCENE

Cut out "scenes" from a New England Village Design Lines and mount on complementary shades of paper or vellum squares. The background color highlights the detail and cutout sections of each sticker.

GREEN HILLS SCENE

Change the color or texture of background paper mounted behind Green Hills Design Lines segments to indicate time of day or season. Tile panels across a larger piece of paper, filmstrip style.

ROCKY MOUNTAIN SCENE

To simulate depth and distance, cut the Rocky Mountains Design Lines into various lengths or widths and mat at different levels on a piece of black paper.

At the Fair

DUPLICATE AN AMUSEMENT PARK FAVORITE

Create custom page accents by building scenes that capture the fun of an exhilarating ride. Accent upper edge of background paper with Design Lines stickers, mounting on self-adhesive foam tape for dimension. Add another DL sticker border to lower edge of background paper. Mount photos and accent with DL stickers. Mount Roller Coaster DL on a 1 x 9" strip of blue cardstock. Use a craft knife and metal straightedge ruler to slice the sticker-laden strip into nine equal 1" squares. Trim any excess overlap from the sides and lower edges of the squares, leaving any overlap on upper edge intact. Mount scenic squares equidistant on a strip of white cardstock that is trimmed with DL stickers. Mount remaining Roller Coaster DL on page for title, top with balloons and letter stickers. Add journaling block accented with food stickers to complete the layout.

Stickers Vellum Color Blocks, Roller Coaster DL, Carnival Food, Primary Active Edges DL, Dots & Stripes DL, Balloons, White Alphabet; **Paper** yellow and white cardstocks; **Other** craft knife; metal straightedge ruler; scissors

Happy 1ˢᵗ Birthday

STACK COLORFUL CAKE LAYERS

Reproduce a party cake several layers high with colorful sticker "frosting." First, mount red cardstock border on background paper. Double mat and mount photos. Cut five equal segments from white cardstock to create cake layers. Decorate each panel with strips of Design Lines stickers across upper and lower edges, trimming off any excess overlap. Add dots, stripes and pen strokes to complete cake layers; assemble and mount askew on page with self-adhesive foam tape for dimension. Top cake with vellum letter stickers topped with candles. Make title with yellow cardstock, blue DL, handmade tag with number sticker and hand-drawn lettering. Finish with photo captions and journaling block.

Stickers Vellum Bubbles, Alphabets, Numbers, Active Edge DL, Twist & Torn DL, Dots & Stripes DL, Primary Panels, Candles; **Paper** white, red and yellow cardstocks; **Other** blue embroidery floss

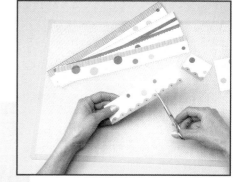

Up Close It may be easiest to cut these extra long Design Lines stickers while they are still on the liner paper. Use a ruler for accurate measurement and cut your borders into the desired sections or lengths.

Optical Illusions

Reflection, distance, depth and viewpoint are just a few of the illusions you can create with a handful of stickers. One key to your success will be finding stickers that are printed in reverse or mirror image. By printing each image in the reverse or opposite direction, stickers can be matched up back-to-back, carry on face-to-face conversations or be reflected as if viewed in a mirror.

Life Is a Journey

CARVE A BAS-RELIEF TITLE

Pop-dotted title letters project from a sticker scene, providing the illusion of bas-relief. Double mat and mount photo. Follow the steps below to create the Design Line sticker border and title. Finish page with letter stickers for remaining portion of title and matted vellum journaling block accented with DL stickers and a single brad fastener.

Stickers Vellum Sky Alphabet, Meadow DL, Classic Alphabet; **Paper** dark green and light green cardstocks, white vellum; **Other** self-adhesive foam spacers; powder; small paintbrush; craft knife; temporary adhesive; brad fastener

How to Create a Bas-Relief Title

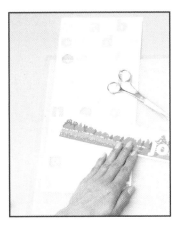

1 While stickers are still on the liner paper, carefully cut out each Alphabet letter you will use in the title. Position and lightly tack each letter on the top of the Design Lines where desired, using a temporary adhesive to hold the letters in place.

2 Carefully cut around each letter using a craft knife. Gently peel up each letter as you cut it and store them on an extra sheet of liner paper.

3 Once all letters are cut out, position DL across the page. Remove the liner paper from the back of each blue vellum letter sticker and place letters in each corresponding negative space resulting from the cutouts in the DL.

4 Put small pieces of self-adhesive foam spacers on the back of each cutout DL letter. You will probably need two to three pieces of spacers per letter. Leave the backing on the foam spacers and gently dust the back of each sticker with powder to neutralize the adhesive. Remove backing from foam spacers and attach each letter on top of the vellum letters.

Our Second Honeymoon

CAST A REFLECTED IMAGE

Create a reflective water scene using mirror-image stickers. Cut a sheet of ivory cardstock for title border panel. Establish a horizon line on lower half of cardstock border, lightly tracing it directly onto the panel or page with a pencil if needed. Build the reflective sticker scene up from the top of the horizon line. Duplicate the scene using the mirror-image stickers (designs printed in the reverse direction); adhering upside down below the horizon line. Line stickers up directly against both sides of the horizon line. Place a cut and torn piece of blue vellum over the lower portion of the sticker scene to mimic water. Add Design Lines stickers to upper and lower edges of title panel and hand draw title lettering. Mount photos and additional DL stickers on page. Complete with a half-circle sticker medallion above photos.

Stickers PW Palm Tree, Giant Birds, Dots & Stripes DL, Grass DL, Rainbow DL, Medallions, Micro Butterflies; **Paper** light green and ivory cardstocks, light blue vellum

Christopher Raids the Chicken Coop

CREATE A COLORFUL KALEIDOSCOPE

Make a unique page accent by stacking mirror-image stickers onto transparency film to create a kaleidoscope design. Begin by dividing page into nine equal sections using Design Lines stickers. Crop and mount photos in seven of the sections. Follow the instructions below to create sticker kaleidoscope. Layer additional animal stickers inside letter stickers to create a custom-coordinated page title.

Stickers Small Farm Animals, Casual Alphabet, Jewel Tone Slivers DL; **Paper** tan cardstock; **Other** transparency film; octagon- or circle-shaped template; brad fastener

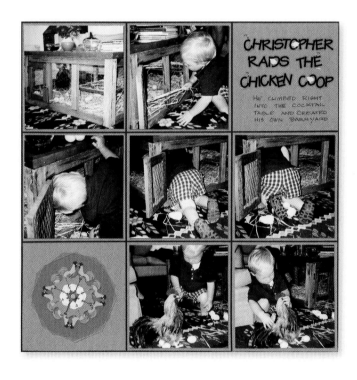

How to Create a Sticker Kaleidoscope

1 Cut two octagonal or circular-shaped discs out of transparency film. Trace the same shape on a scrap piece of cardstock and draw eight equally spaced lines through the center of the paper circle for placement pattern. Layer one transparency disc over pattern and place roosters evenly on lines in a circular fashion, positioning so beaks and tails touch. In the same manner, stack hens and chicks on second disc, placing toward center of pattern. Layer and attach kaleidoscope discs to page using a brad fastener. Spin the discs to see the kaleidoscope in action!

Weaving With Stickers

We weave baskets, rugs and textiles, so why not try it with stickers and paper? Weaving strips of paper decorated with stickers brings a textured dimension to your album pages. Use these weaving techniques to create subtle and structured journal panels, page borders and backgrounds.

Baby

WEAVE A SOFT PLAID PAGE BORDER

Incorporate pastel paper and Design Lines stickers into a woven design for a soft look, and experiment with bolder colors for a more outspoken approach. Start with a yellow cardstock background. Follow the steps below to create the woven page border. Mount photos and complete page with title made from deckle-cut cardstock squares topped with letter stickers. Complete journaling on a piece of vellum. Attach to top of woven section, using button stickers backed with self-adhesive foam spacers.

Stickers Soft Shade Sliver DL, Buttons, Twilight Alphabet; **Paper** light blue, salmon pink and white cardstocks; white vellum; **Other** paper trimmer or craft knife and metal straightedge ruler; removable artist's tape; decorative scissors

How to Weave a Page Border

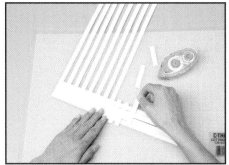

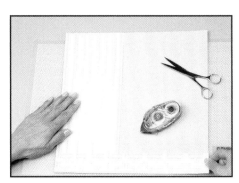

1 Cut fourteen ⅜ x 12" strips of light blue cardstock. Place two narrow Design Lines sticker borders on the outside edges of four strips. Place a single sticker border down the center of ten 12" long strips; cut two of the ten strips into 2" long pieces.

2 Tack the four strips down horizontally on your work surface with removable artist's tape. Carefully weave the eight 12" long strips vertically into the left hand side of the four horizontal strips, leaving space between each of the vertical strips. Follow with the smaller 2" sections to finish the base of your woven piece. Trim off ¼" excess overlap.

3 Mat the vertical woven strips with white cardstock and move the woven piece to your page, trimming off any excess overlap.

Spring Grasses

TUCK THEME STICKERS INTO WEAVING

For a sweet and earthy accent, create a page border that implies the hint of a basket or a slat fence with grasses poking through. Start with a yellow background page (an 8 x 8" page shown). Mat and mount photo. Add letter sticker title. Photocopy and size pattern on page 109 onto a sheet of 8½ x 11" white cardstock. Cut pattern on interior lines to create slots for weaving. Attach white, slit cardstock panel across lower edge of background paper. Insert sections cut from wheat stickers through alternating paper strips and adhere, creating woven effect without the work. Add journaling to complete page.

Stickers Wheat, Classic Alphabet; **Paper** Mrs. Grossman's Buttered Corn and Just Plain Vanilla Ribbed cardstocks; **Other** pattern on page 109

Cute

INCORPORATE HIDDEN JOURNALING INTO MOCK WEAVE

Mimic weaving with translucent vellum stickers that borrow colors from the photos. Place wide, vellum Design Lines stickers ¼" apart down the vertical edge of background page. Run additional borders, in contrasting colors and widths, in a horizontal direction across page, capturing a vellum pocket beneath the horizontal stripes. The translucent stickers create the look of weaving. Add vellum panels atop sticker strips and mount photos. Make page title with vellum sticker letters accented with small sections cut from daisy stickers and freehand journaling. Finish with a daisy sticker medallion on envelope and journaling tucked inside.

Stickers Powder Alphabet, Daisy, Vellum Rainbow DL, Vellum Ribbon DL; **Paper** white cardstock, pink and yellow vellums

Stickers Beneath Vellum

What's not to love about vellum? It's so versatile! Use simple vellum overlays to soften bold, bright stickers or stark black journaling. Vellum can also be used to create an illusion of distance or to fade a sticker art scene to the background allowing the viewers' eyes to focus on the photos.

I've Fallen for You

CREATE THE ILLUSION OF DEPTH

Layer vellum, cardstock and stickers to bring depth and implied perspective to your scrapbook pages. Start with a light green background page. Cut a 3½" white cardstock border panel for page. Decorate the border with leaf and border stickers. Tear a piece of iridescent or flecked vellum and place it diagonally across the center of border panel. Tear green vellum and add at opposite corners. Cut cream vellum 1" shorter than white cardstock; center and adhere over border panel. Layer additional leaf stickers on top, shifting leaves slightly to create shadow effect. If you wish, eliminate cardstock and work strictly with layered vellum for a softer approach as illustrated in the title panel. Mount photos accented with Design Lines stickers, layered leaf and letter sticker title and torn vellum journaling panel to finish layout.

Stickers Vellum Fall Leaves, Twist & Torn DL, White Alphabet; **Paper** celery and white cardstocks, iridescent or glitter-flecked vellum, cream and light green vellums

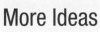

More Ideas

MAKE A MAGNIFYING GLASS

Stickers Vellum Leaves, Ladybugs

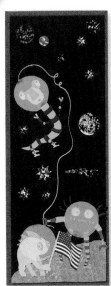

FASHION SOME OUT-OF-THIS-WORLD HEADGEAR

Stickers Endorfuns, SP Solar System, Small Flag, Primary Slivers DL

COMPOSE A SHEER CURTAIN SCENE

Stickers Puppies, Bathtub

DEPICT A SNOWY WINDOW SCENE

Stickers Snow Tree, Winterscape DL, Small Santa, Primary DL

Grammy's Candy Shop

DESIGN MILK-GLASS CANISTERS

A vellum overlay softens jars of colorful Christmas candy, providing an illusion that stickers are stored safely inside milk-glass jars. Begin by accenting page edges with lacy Design Lines stickers. Mat photo, edge with DL stickers and mount on page. Trim long journaling panel with DL stickers, photos and candy stickers. Freehand draw jars on scraps of white cardstock; cut out pieces. Layer jars with candy stickers and top each jar with a piece of white vellum trimmed to fit. Top each jar with a "lid" cut from the tan, metallic silver or gray cardstock scraps. Use pieces of remaining candy stickers and hand-drawn lettering to create page title.

Stickers Henry's Lace DL, Christmas Candy, Soft Shade Sliver DL; **Paper** Mrs. Grossman's Sage Advice Ribbed cardstock and dark sage and white cardstocks; tan, silver metallic or gray paper scraps; white vellum

Oahu

TUCK STICKER FISH SAFELY BEHIND ROLLING WAVES

Bring an aquatic scene to life with sea creature stickers, torn vellum and handmade "sea foam." Adhere trimmed blue cardstock onto background page. Tear blue vellum and brown paper to create water and sand. Build an ocean scene on trimmed, light green cardstock and layer the blue and brown paper over it, torn edges up. Tuck fish stickers behind water and starfish and grass on the sand. Create sea foam by rubbing white chalk across the torn edges of the brown paper. Lightly coat the torn blue edges with glue and apply glitter and tiny glass marbles. Repeat torn edge technique in title panel and medallion using vellum Water Design Lines. Mount photos and add journaling to finish page.

Stickers Sky Alphabet, VL Water DL, Sea Creatures, OP Sea Life, Grass DL; **Paper** blue, white and light green cardstock, brown sand-textured paper, blue vellum; **Other** liquid adhesive; tiny glass marbles (Halcraft); white glitter; white chalk (Craf-T)

Adding Sticker Dimension

Take your sticker art from flat to fabulous with a small piece of self-adhesive foam tape. Use dimension to frame photos or journaling and add detail and depth to sticker accents. But don't forget to powder the back of each design before you stick! A light dusting of powder makes sure your sticker art stays "popped up" off the page.

Hydrangea

BUILD A 3-D FLORAL LATTICE

It's easy to make realistic latticework to contain floral sticker art by attaching it to a page with self-adhesive foam tape or spacers. Create even more of a 3-D effect by stacking hydrangea blossoms on top of each other. Start by adding a 2¼" lavender border, accented with Design Lines stickers, on background page. Accent photos with additional DL stickers; mount on page. Follow the steps below to create latticework. Add letter sticker title. Finish with DL accented journaling block accented with floral stickers and a faux crystal accent.

Stickers Hydrangea, Multi Metallic Sliver DL, Soft Shade DL, Soft Shade Sliver DL, White Alphabet, Hydrangea DL; **Paper** Mrs. Grossman's Twilight and Lavender Sachet Ribbed cardstocks; **Other** self-adhesive foam tape or spacers; Mrs. Grossman's Opal Crystal Accents

How to Build a Lattice

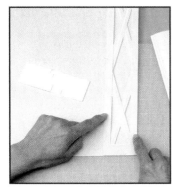

1 Cut four ½ x 6½" paper strips. Accent strips with Design Lines stickers down the center of each strip. Layer and crisscross the paper strips and adhere behind a 2¼ x 12" paper frame to form lattice. Accent frame edges with additional DL stickers. Mount entire arrangement on page using small pieces of self-adhesive foam tape.

2 Decorate lattice and frame with leaves and individual blossoms cut from Hydrangea stickers.

3 Identify sections of art where you wish to add dimension. Cut matching stickers from the Hydrangeas. Place small pieces of self-adhesive foam tape on the back of each sticker, leaving the tape liner in place. Lightly dust the back of each sticker with powder or cornstarch to neutralize the adhesive and make sure sticker will stay "popped" up off page.

4 Position "popped" stickers on top of their "twins," attaching to page with foam tape. Cut out individual blossoms or sections and pop on larger arrangements for finely detailed dimension.

The Great Outdoors

ADD PERSPECTIVE TO A STICKER SCENE

You're not seeing double, you're just adding more depth and dimension by incorporating foam tape behind certain elements in an entire sticker scene. Start by mounting photos on background paper. Place a few cloud stickers and a Rocky Mountain Design Lines sticker across lower edge of page to begin the scenic border. Crop elements from additional cloud and mountain stickers and layer directly on the identical designs, sandwiching self-adhesive foam tape pieces or spacers between the sticker layers. "Pop" laser-cut tree stickers directly on top of your sticker picture. Complete the page by adding title sign made from wood-grain paper and framed journaling block. "Pop" a few parts of the title panel to make your words stand out as well.

Stickers Rocky Mountain DL, Fir Tree; Paper Mrs. Grossman's Buttered Corn Ribbed cardstock, wood patterned paper (Golden Oak), cream cardstock; Other self-adhesive foam spacers or foam tape; powder

The Huntington

GIVE ARCHITECTURAL FEATURES DEPTH

Build an alcove or frame artwork and photos with architectural stickers that are given a physical presence by you. For journaling panel, frame blue vellum with sticker treetops and Greco border. Construct alcove from black and tan papers and position on right edge of panel. Place tiny pieces of self-adhesive foam spacers on the back of statue and columns. Lightly powder the back of stickers and attach to panel using self-adhesive foam spacers. Cut section of branches from tree and overlap on top of existing tree using more foam tape adhesive to create overhang. For photo frame, mount photo on page. Decorate top and bottom edges with architectural details placed flush with page. "Pop" columns on each side of photo using self-adhesive foam spacers. Mount remaining photos in place and add letter sticker title to complete page.

Stickers Greco Columns DL, Park, Oak Tree, Classic Alphabet, Rome; Paper Mrs. Grossman's Atmosphere Ribbed cardstock and light blue, black, tan and light green paper scraps; Other self-adhesive foam spacers or foam tape; powder

Sticker Collage

Sticker bits and pieces—whether cut from scratch or saved from scraps—make for elegant and easy collage. Arranged in clusters, cut or torn into shapes to be hand-pieced together or layered directly on top of each other, stickers can be collaged in many different ways to fit any scrapbook page theme.

Mr. & Mrs. J.T. Ingram

LAYER A SENTIMENTAL STICKER COLLAGE

Various theme-related stickers join together beneath a vellum panel to create a timeless and elegant photo mat collage. First, mount printed paper diagonally across background page; trim off any excess overlap. Trim vellum paper to 7½ x 10½" in size. Adhere trimmed and torn stickers face-up on the back of vellum in an eye-pleasing fashion; trim away any excess overlap at edges. Accent front of vellum mat with additional lace, floral, button and Design Lines stickers, trimming at edges as needed. Center and mount vellum on page; add photo. Use a small piece of foam tape to attach caption panel to top of collage.

Stickers Vellum Medallions, Ferns, Hydrangea DL, Buttons, Rosebuds, Lace Medallions, Soft Shade Sliver DL; **Paper** pink cardstock, script patterned paper (K & Company), translucent vellum

More Ideas

CREATE A DELICATE FLORAL COLLAGE TAG

Stickers Vellum Medallions, Vellum Streamers, Hollyhock, Small Reflections Hearts; Mrs. Grossman's Rose Crystal Accents

COLLAGE A SWEET SENTIMENT

Stickers Brocade Heart, Silk Bow, Lace Medallions, Silverware, Small Reflections Hearts

COMMEMORATE A SPECIAL EVENT WITH A MEDALLION COLLAGE

Stickers Love Stamps, Micro Hearts, Alphabitsy

Sonoma

COMPILE A STICKER-MOSAIC COLLAGE

Borrow elements from your photographs to create a colorful collage. Place a collection of letter stickers for title and image stickers randomly on two white cardstock border panels; trim any excess overlap. Use scissors or craft knife to carefully cut colored vellum stickers into "shards." Adhere each individual shard in random, abstract mosaic fashion on title and border panels, placing around the borders' previously placed sticker images and lettering. Repeat sticker mosaics at the top of each journaling panel for continuity. Mount all elements, including photos, in place on page.

Stickers Vellum Color Blocks, Sky Alphabet, Giant Birds, Oak Tree, Washington DC, Palm Tree, Stagecoach, Rose Garden; **Paper** cream and white cardstocks; **Other** small scissors or a craft knife

Mexico

COLLAGE PAGE CORNERS FOR IMPACT

This is a great way to use theme stickers in collage fashion for subtle visual appeal on a page. Start by cropping theme stickers to fit on metallic paper squares, allowing some sticker edges to purposely overlap the square edges. Arrange and adhere sticker accent squares around four corners of album page, layering collage style with additional theme stickers. Mount 10 x 10" complementary-colored cardstock diagonally askew on background paper exposing corner sticker collages and add Design Line stickers to edge of paper; trim off excess overlap. Mat photos and journaling on white cardstock trimmed with decorative scissors; mount on page. Use remaining pieces of cut stickers on edges of journaling panel. Adhere page title sticker on photo using self-adhesive foam spacers for lift.

Stickers Mexico, Palm Tree, Greco Columns DL, Vellum Cool Metallic Squares; **Paper** Mrs. Grossman's Atmosphere Ribbed cardstock, white and tan cardstocks; **Other** decorative scissors

Sticker Shaker Boxes

Purchase ready-made windows and boxes or construct your own using our simple techniques. Once filled with sand, glitter, beads or colorful stickers and playfully tossed about, our childhood fascination with holiday snow globes quickly returns.

Lions, Legos, Bears, Oh My!

ACCENT SHAKER TAGS WITH STICKERS

Shaker boxes are fun page accents made visually intriguing when decorated with theme and letter stickers. Begin with matted background paper. Crop, mat and mount photos. Follow the steps below to create shaker box tags and mount on page. Add matted journaling block to finish layout.

Stickers PW Alphabet, Lion, Panda; **Paper** dark green and tan cardstocks; clear tiny glass marbles; page protector or transparency film; self-adhesive foam tape or spacers; brown fibers

How to Build Shaker Box Tags

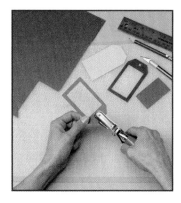

1 Cut a total of eight tags from cardstock. Punch or cut a rectangle from the center of four of the tags. Punch holes in tag ends.

2 Attach clear insert, cut from page protector or transparency film, inside each window to serve as a cover. Adhere stickers on tag backgrounds and foregrounds, attaching directly to clear insert.

3 Turn tag over and cover each edge with foam tape, trimming as needed to fit around inner window rectangles. Pour a small amount of sand, glitter or tiny glass marbles onto back of tag window in between the self-adhesive foam tape. Include back-to-back stickers, charms or other items you wish to "float" inside the window.

4 Assemble shaker tag boxes by securely adhering tag backgrounds to window foregrounds. Tie tag ends with fibers.

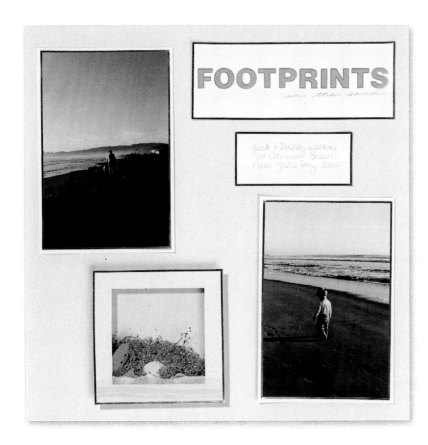

Footprints

STORE MEMENTOS AND STICKERS IN A SHAKER BOX FRAME

Shaker boxes provide an interesting showcase for memorabilia. Adding theme stickers inside the shaker box reinforces the page theme. First mat and mount photos and adhere. Following the instructions on the previous page, cut cardstock and a piece of foam core to desired box size. Punch a square window from center; attach a trimmed piece of clear acetate or transparency film to backside of window. Turn window over and cover each inner edge with self-adhesive foam tape, trimming as needed to fit around window. Pour a small amount of sand and back-to-back sea life stickers in center of window between foam tape. Center and adhere box backing securely in place; mount shaker box on page. Complete the page with letter sticker title and journaling block.

Stickers OP Sea Life, Metallic Sliver DL, Twilight Alphabet, Vellum Water DL; **Paper** aqua and blue-green cardstocks; **Other** ½" thick foam core board; page protector or transparency film; mega square punch or square template; sand

Honey Run

ENCAPSULATE AN ORGANIC SHAKER SCENE

Take a shaker box shortcut by attaching acetate to paper panel with foam tape, eliminating the need for box front. Begin by cutting a page protector or transparency film and cardstock backing in 4½ x 3½" rectangles. Mount cardstock rectangle on lower corner of page; trim with self-adhesive foam tape around all edges and fill inner space with dried, pressed flowers. Center and mount clear "window" over filled cardstock rectangle and secure in place. Apply Perch Woodpecker sticker on right-hand edge of window. Border remaining three edges with leaf stickers, overlapping to add fullness and create frame. Mat and mount photos and letter sticker title. Freehand cut covered bridge journaling block and mount on page.

Stickers Studio Line Song Birds, Celery Alphabet, Scrap Metal Blocks; **Paper** green, cream and brown cardstocks; **Other** pressed flowers and leaves

Sticker Shadow Boxes
A current trend toward embellishments encourages many of us to build pages "out" higher and higher, layer after layer. Here you will find a more "inward" approach, using foam core board and foam tape. You can showcase tiny treasures or photos in shadow boxes or recessed alcoves. Both flat stickers and dimensional objects are protected in structured page frames, offering a compartmentalized approach to scrapbooking.

Mott

BUILD A FAUX PRINTER'S TRAY

Re-create a classic printer's tray shadow box to house timeless photos and tiny sticker treasures. Begin with two shades of brown cardstock, using the darker paper for the bottom layer and the lighter paper for the top layer of the shadow box. Follow the steps below to create the shadow box. Place charms, stickers and accessories in each of the compartments, using small pieces of foam tape behind the stickers to add dimension. Fashion a page title in similar manner using letter and block stickers. Add a lighter or darker border around the interior of each compartment for more depth. Mount photos in place and finish with freehand-cut bookplate for journaling.

Stickers Buttons, Lewis & Clark, PW Leaves, Ivy DL, Soft Shade DL, Scalloped Lace DL, Metallic Vellum Color Blocks; **Paper** tan and dark brown cardstocks; **Other** 1/8" thick foam core board same size as cardstock; square and rectangular shape templates (optional); craft knife; metal straightedge ruler; temporary adhesive; metal charms; brad fasteners

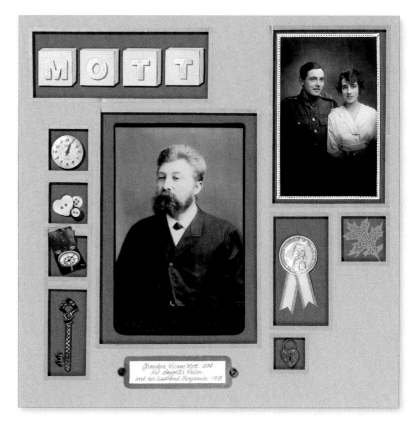

How to Build a Shadow Box

1 Use a pencil and metal straightedge ruler to lightly freehand draw square and rectangle shapes on tan cardstock in a manner that will provide a visually appealing presentation. You can also use shape templates to trace the shapes. Use a craft knife and metal straightedge ruler to cut out the shapes.

2 Layer the tan cardstock over foam core board, lining up all edges and holding in place with a temporary adhesive. Use a pencil to lightly trace the shapes onto the foam core and cut out.

3 Lining up all page and foam core edges and openings, sandwich together the cut tan cardstock, the cut foam core and the dark brown cardstock, adhering together permanently. Frame each compartment with a neutral Design Lines border.

Under the Sea

FILL AN AQUARIUM SHADOW BOX

Tear a peek-through faux ocean to create an underwater look at sea creatures—including human ones! First, adhere stickers across background cardstock in random fashion; cover entire page with blue vellum. Position photos and paper journaling and memorabilia panels toward center of page, framing each with a Design Lines sticker border. Carefully tear center out of blue cardstock to create a frame and mount in place over 1/8" thick foam core frame cut to page size; adhere over background scene. Tuck additional stickers inside edge of torn shadow-box frame. Use small pieces of foam tape on the back of the stickers to add dimension. Finish with letter sticker and Vellum Water Design Lines page title.

Stickers OP Sea Life, OP Fish, OP Coral, Aqua Alphabet, Vellum Water DL, Casual Alphabet; **Paper** light blue vellum, cream and ocean blue cardstocks; **Other** sea glass and sand dollars (found)

Tamari

ENCASE A COLORFUL SCHOOL COLLECTION

Bring the classroom to life with a shadow box filled with school photos, stickers and even a crayon box! Begin by matting photos, accenting them with Design Lines stickers and mounting on background. Add stickers, a tiny piece of cut notebook paper for journaling and a pencil. Construct the crayon box from yellow and green cardstocks. Crop window into front of box and attach cut page protector or transparency film inside to create a shaker box. Cut 10½ x 10½" square from center of yellow cardstock; color block outside edges with stickers and red paper slices to create a page frame. Mount frame to background using two layers of foam tape for depth.

Stickers School DL, Alphabitsy, Classroom Stuff, Primary Slivers DL; **Paper** green, blue, yellow, red and teal cardstocks; lined notebook paper; **Other** multicolor pencils, broken into pieces and sharpened; small yellow #2 pencil; page protector or transparency film; self-adhesive foam tape

Cropping & Punching Stickers

Crop and cut stickers to cover precut paper mats and frames. Punch paper shapes to hand-piece geometric borders or backgrounds for pages. Combine stickers and punched shapes for custom backgrounds and patterns to use on a variety of pages where existing artwork is hard to find.

Jenni

CROP CUSTOMIZED FRAMES

Pastel heart stickers layered and overlapped across cardstock frames create a custom pattern. Begin by layering title and journaling frames cut from white cardstock. Layer stickers in an eye-pleasing fashion, overlapping each other and edges of frames where desired. Turn frames over and use scissors to trim away excess sticker overlap. Edge frames in Design Lines stickers and back with letter sticker title and journaling on vellum; adhere on page. Mount matted photos to finish page.

Stickers Vellum Hearts, Celery Alphabet, Soft Shade Sliver DL;
Paper Mrs. Grossman's Strawberry Shake and Celery Sticks Ribbed cardstock, white cardstock, Mrs. Grossman's Strawberry Shake vellum

More Ideas

CROP AN ACTIVE SPORTS SCENE
Stickers Girls' and Boys' Soccer, Soccer Gear

CUT UP A WILD PARTY
Stickers Ext. Wild Animals, Birthday Party, Giant Presents, Happy Birthday, Micro Music, Birthday Cake

CROP A GEOMETRIC BACKDROP
Stickers Vellum Metallic Blocks, New York

Busy Busy Bee

COMBINE PUNCHED PAPER WITH STICKERS

Tile a honeycomb pattern behind the page title using a hexagon paper punch. Mount black cardstock paper slices on yellow cardstock for upper and lower page borders. Punch several yellow hexagons and arrange along upper border. Dance letter stickers across a sheet of vellum for title; attach to page with brad fasteners. Mount photos on page; add bee stickers and pen stroke details. Complete with punched and layered paper hexagons mounted at left of matted journaling.

Stickers Bee, Casual Alphabet, Classroom Stuff, Playground; **Paper** Mrs. Grossman's Buttered Corn Ribbed cardstock, black paper and white cardstocks, black polka-dot paper (Paper Patch), translucent white vellum; **Other** hexagon paper punches in small, medium and large sizes; small brad fasteners

Point Reyes

CROP PHOTO AND STICKER SCENE BLOCKS

Sticker scenes accent a page of cropped squares, rectangles and blocks, squeezing many photos onto a single page. Use a page template or freehand crop photos. Build sticker scenes by placing trees and shrubs between layers of torn Metallic Blocks stickers. Add birds to foreground and trim scenes to fit in squares. Position title on white vellum overlay.

Stickers Sapphire Alphabet, Oak Tree, Game Birds, Scrap Metal Blocks, Marsh Life; **Paper** dark brown and light brown cardstocks, white vellum

Building Interactive Pockets
Tuck a journaling panel inside one of these creative pocket ideas. Whether it's constructed from woven, folded or sheer paper, the pocket will add a touch of interactive surprise to any scrapbook page.

Easter

TUCK JOURNALING IN A BASKET POCKET

Hide journaling with sticker grass and eggs for a clever Easter surprise. First, mount photos on page and mat with Design Lines stickers. Follow the steps below to create the basket and grass border. Layer foam tape and sections of grass to make a dimensional border. Decorate top edge of journal panel and slip it inside the basket pocket. Weave paper strips in similar fashion to create title block fence; add letter stickers on paper blocks trimmed with decorative scissors to complete page.

Stickers Grass DL, Easter Eggs, Lilac Alphabet, Rainbow DL, Sheer Pink Ribbon; **Paper** celery and pink papers, white cardstock; **Other** self-adhesive foam tape; craft knife; decorative scissors

How to Make a Woven Basket

1 Cut a piece of cardstock 2" wider and 2" higher than your desired journaling panel. Draw a horizontal line 1" from the bottom of cardstock. Cut vertical slits across the paper at ½" intervals up to, but not across the line. Cut another piece of paper into ⁷⁄₁₆ x 5" strips. Weave the strips through the slits in the paper. When woven panel is complete, trim top edge and side edges to fit space on page.

2 For dimensional grass, carefully fold the bottom of the Design Lines up ½". Peel the liner back from the top of the sticker (the bottom remains on the liner) and powder the back of the blades of grass to neutralize the adhesive. To create the dimensional border pictured above, trim lengths of the DL to various heights and layer on bottom of page, tucking in small pieces of foam tape between each layer of grass.

3 Attach dimensional grass to top edge of woven panel and adhere sides and lower edge of basket to page, leaving upper edge open for journaling insert.

4 Crop a journaling panel to fit inside basket, accenting with back-to-back grass and egg stickers across the upper edge of the panel. Cut basket handle out of paper.

Fun in the Sun

MAKE A PEEK-A-BOO JOURNALING POCKET

Use translucent vellum and stickers to create a see-through journaling panel. Mount blue vellum across lower three-fourths of page; top with cardstock and sticker border strip. Create title with grass and letter stickers; accent with bee and flower stickers adhered with self-adhesive foam spacers for depth. Measure and fold vellum to create pocket. Adhere to page using side and bottom edges. Decorate top edge of pocket with paper and sticker border. Cut journaling panel to fit inside pocket. Place grass or sticker border across top edge of panel, powdering the backs of the stickers extended over top edge; accent with additional floral stickers. Mount photos in place to finish page.

Stickers Grass DL, Sky Alphabet, Twist & Tom DL, Bees, African Daisies; **Paper** light blue cardstock, Mrs. Grossman's Twilight Ribbed cardstock, light blue and white vellums; **Other** self-adhesive foam tape or spacers

A View of the Garden

LANDSCAPE A TRI-FOLD JOURNALING POCKET

Continue a photo theme with a custom-coordinated journaling panel. Begin by mounting double-matted photos on page. Embellish upper and lower page edges with Design Lines stickers. Make the torn paper tri-fold journaling pocket and adhere. Complete with sticker medallion and letter sticker title.

Stickers Silver Deco Lace DL, Lavender, Hollyhock, PW Alphabet; **Paper** blue, light blue and green cardstocks; **Other** self-adhesive foam tape or spacers

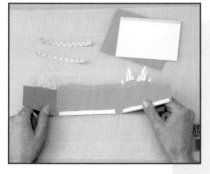

Up Close To make the tri-fold pocket, tear the top edge of a strip of paper. Score and tri-fold strip to desired size of journaling insert. Decorate each panel of pocket with stickers, powdering the sticker parts that extend over the top of panel to prevent sticking. Attach thin strips of foam tape to the middle and right-hand panels. Fold each pocket panel inward, starting with the left side. Glue pocket to a solid panel of paper and decorate journaling insert before placing on page.

Memorabilia Pockets
Whimsical, witty and even winsome pockets store souvenirs, keepsakes and family history to complete the story on your album page. Crafted from paper and stickers, these patterns and techniques can be used over and over again to help keep your memories intact.

New York, New York
RE-CREATE A TRAVEL-WARDROBE FAVORITE

Pull those souvenirs tucked safely in your travel pocket and place them in faux denim pockets for permanent safekeeping. Follow the steps below to create the side border pocket panel. Double mat photos; mount on page. Cut out paper pocket liner using denim pocket sticker as pattern and cutting paper to fit just inside the yellow seams. Powder top edge of sticker pocket to neutralize the adhesive; adhere to top of paper liner. Use the remaining outside edges to attach pocket sticker on page. Tuck memorabilia inside pocket. Attach a tiny pocket to the top of original pocket to hold coins or tokens. Trim the small pocket shape from another sticker and line with paper following steps below. Add title and journaling block.

Stickers Jean Pocket, Jeans & Bandana DL, New York; **Paper** denim, black and Mrs. Grossman's Grey Day Ribbed cardstock; **Other** double-sided adhesive tape

How to Create a Memorabilia Pocket

1 Use a craft knife and metal straightedge ruler to cut a 3" slit across upper edge of denim paper border.

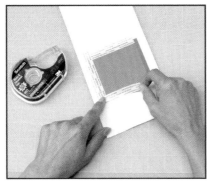

2 Construct paper liner or sleeve out of lightweight paper and attach to back of denim paper border, holding in place with tape adhesive.

3 Accent border with rivet and seam stickers. Tuck in memorabilia or color copies of memorabilia, inserting through slit. Mount denim pocket border on left side of cardstock background.

Caitlyn Marie

ANNOUNCE A BIRTH IN STYLE

Tuck baby's birth announcement, locks of hair or extra photos into a pretty pocket made from patterned paper and stickers. Accent the lower edge of cardstock background with Design Lines stickers. Cut and fold patterned-paper pocket flaps inside; adhere pocket on page. Drape a sticker charm bracelet on the pocket by stacking stickers with self-adhesive foam spacers; add Crystal Accents. Tuck announcement in pocket. Add matted photos and title to complete page.

Stickers OP Hearts, VL Ribbon DL, Pink Linen Ribbon DL, OP Stars, Baby's Things, OP Sun Moon & Stars; **Paper** Petal Pink paper (DMD), Mrs. Grossman's Strawberry Shake Ribbed cardstock, lavender striped paper (Paper Garden), citron green paper; **Other** Mrs. Grossman's Aquamarine Crystal Accents; self-adhesive foam spacers

Mom

MAKE A USEFUL PORTFOLIO POCKET

Portfolio pockets are the perfect pocket for college and career scrapbook pages. Fold a 9¾ x 11" paper to 7 x 5½", creating a 2¾" flap across the bottom edge. Trim inside flaps to resemble portfolio or folder. Adhere outer edges of flaps to folder to hold contents inside. Reduce and photocopy school report cards and journals to a smaller size to fit inside the folder. Use dyes and pastels to age color copies and binder paper, giving them a dated look. Mount matted photo on front of portfolio and decorate page with sticker borders and corners cut from paper. Add letter sticker nameplate to complete page.

Stickers Patterned Heart DL, PW Alphabet; **Paper** blue, green, black cardstocks, lined notebook paper; **Other** dyes and pastels (Dr. Ph. Martin's)

Sticker Pop-Up Pages

Borrow a papercrafting technique from your childhood to make playful pop-up pages. Use cardstock and heavyweight paper for simple spirals or a series of folded panels to make your photos and journaling jump right off the page. Use stickers to add a delightful touch to pop-ups.

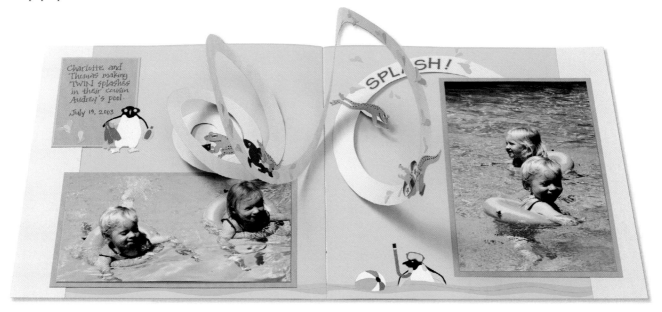

Splash

SPRING A SPIRAL STICKER POP-UP

A page-turning pop-up always creates a fun element of surprise to any scrapbook page spread. Start with paper and sticker borders along edges of two 8 x 8" scrapbook pages. Turn spread over and tape pages together on backside to bind spread together. Pages should easily fold backward and forward. Follow the steps below to create spiral pop-up. Accent the spiral pop-up with back-to-back animal and splash stickers. Finish with letter sticker title on spiral and sticker-accented journaling block.

Stickers Casual Alphabet, Frogs, Penguins, Crocodiles, Swimming Gear, Water DL **Paper** blue, light blue, gray blue cardstocks; **Other** pattern on page 109; double-sided tape adhesive; scissors

How to Make a Spiral Pop-Up

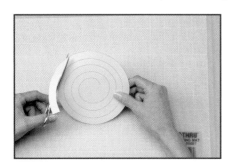

1 Photocopy and enlarge pattern on page 109, sizing to fit scrapbook page spread and photocopying onto cardstock. Use scissors to cut out the spiral.

2 Position your spiral on left side of spread, attaching the inner end of the spiral to page with permanent adhesive.

3 Stretch spiral across to right side of spread and hold other end at desired position. Before attaching, close pages to make sure that spiral will fold flat when spread is closed.

London

BUILD AN ARCHITECTURAL FOLDED-PANEL POP-UP

Three sticker paper panels take a European adventure three-dimensional, letting the photographs and sticker scenery share the story. Turn two 8 x 8" scrapbook pages over and tape pages together on backside to bind spread together. Pages should easily fold backward and forward. Mat, layer and mount photos and journaling block on the two-page spread. Follow the steps below to build the three-layer folded pop-up panels.

Stickers London, Pathways DL, Ocean DL, Sapphire Alphabet; **Paper** Mrs. Grossman's Grey Day Ribbed cardstock and blue cardstocks; **Other** three patterns on page 108

How to Build a Folded Panel Pop-Up

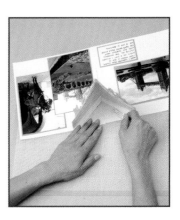

1 Photocopy and enlarge the three patterns on page 108, sizing to fit scrapbook page spread and photocopying onto cardstock. Cut out paper pieces. Decorate the top edge of each panel with stickers, building the scene, using back-to-back sticker designs or powder the back of single stickers to neutralize the adhesive.

2 Gently fold the panels and flaps as indicated by dotted lines on pattern. The flaps on the largest panel will fold back while the smaller panels will fold forward. Attach middle panel to back of largest panel, front sides facing outward, gluing or taping flaps securely ½" from top edge. Make sure that folds in center of each panel are in exact alignment.

3 Attach smallest panel to backside of middle panel, gluing or taping flaps securely ¼" from top edge, with front sides facing outward. Make sure that folds in center of each panel are in exact alignment.

4 Making sure flaps are folded backward, attach one flap of largest panel directly to each album page. The panels will form a triangular shape at top of pages. Gently close pages, making sure panels collapse and fold to middle of spread before adhering permanently in place.

Animating Stickers

Put your pages in motion with ingenious pull-tabs and string techniques, bringing your cheerful sticker friends and vehicles to life. An engineering degree is not required, but a little imagination is.

Happy Fall

FASHION A SWINGIN' STICKER SCARECROW

Accent your artwork with a movable element reminiscent of childhood toys. Try this technique with any "full body" sticker character. Start with a color-block background. Add matted photo as shown. Follow the steps below to create the movable character corner accent. Use small pieces of foam tape to support and secure the scarecrow's torso and head to the page over a cornfield sticker background. Your scarecrow will perform his silly dance against the cornfield backdrop with a simple pull of the strings. Finish page with handwritten and letter sticker title and journaling block.

Stickers Build-A-Scarecrow, Spice Alphabet; **Paper** tan, rust and brown cardstocks; **Other** embroidery threads or string; 1/8" round hand punch; brad fasteners; self-adhesive foam tape or spacers

How to Build a Swinging Scarecrow

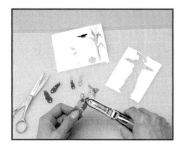

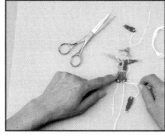

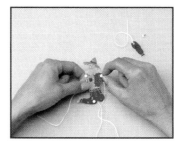

1 Adhere scarecrow stickers on heavy cardstock for strength and use scissors to cut out the pieces following exact outline of stickers. Punch small holes in torso and limb stickers.

2 Tie a small segment of embroidery threads through hole in each arm and leg. Thread through torso as well.

3 Place a small brad through each hole on the front of the scarecrow, attaching arms and legs behind torso.

4 Gather strings into a bundle behind the scarecrow, creating a pull string between scarecrow's legs; build a pull-tab from paper and attach at end of strings. Use additional pieces of foam tape to attach scarecrow to page, placing tape behind head and lower torso.

Go Kart Kids

DRIVE A SLIDE-PULL BORDER

A pull-tab propels this sticker vehicle across the bottom of a scrapbook page with all of the mechanics cleverly camouflaged in the sticker scene and behind the album page. Trim blue cardstock to 11½" square. Follow the steps below to create the scenic pull-tab border. Add clouds freehand cut from white cardstock. Mount double-matted photo. Finish page with letter sticker title and journaling on clouds; mat with white cardstock.

Stickers Yellow Alphabet, Green Hills DL, Grass, Pathways DL, School, Custom Cars; **Paper** white and light blue cardstocks, yellow vellum; **Other** two tiny ⅛" brad fasteners; one standard ¼" brad fastener; ⅛" hole punch; metal straightedge ruler; craft knife

How to Create a Sliding Pull-Tab

1 Build the sticker scenery across bottom of trimmed blue cardstock. Use a metal straightedge ruler and craft knife to cut a 4¾" horizontal slit across the center of border. Cut a ⅞" vertical slit on right hand side of page, leaving a ¾" margin of space between horizontal and vertical slits.

2 Fold or cut a 6¼" long by ⅝" high pull-tab from heavy cardstock or paper. Decorate with stickers and punch small hole ½" in from left edge. Construct car out of stickers, carefully cutting it out from cardstock and punching small holes at tire centers. Top ⅛" brads with tire stickers to create moving wheels and attach to vehicle.

3 Attach car in front of slot and left edge of pull-tab (not visible or shown). Rest pull-tab in back of horizontal slot on page, using larger brad to hold both pull-tab and car in place.

4 Align the car at right edge, threading pull-tab through vertical slot, resting it on front of page. Gently push pull-tab to far left end of slot to move car forward.

CHINO
AIRCRAFT MUSEUM

We enjoyed seeing all the vintage aircraft.

The P-40 Warhawk, with its painted face, is my favorite.

sisters

AUDRI

KARI

Home from college for the holidays, they were showing their new parkas from Santa.
2002

fond memories

As the girls get older I can see them becoming good friends as well as sisters. When when driving in the car with their friends I get a glimpse of what their friendships will become.

2003

remember this

CHAPTER THREE
Embellishing Stickers

Scrapbooking with stickers focuses on helping you get your photographs and your story down on the page. We've shown you how to use stickers to help communicate and interact with the events on each album page. Now we're ready to take your stickers and sticker art to the next level!

Embellish your pages by enhancing and adding elaborate details. We've packed this chapter full of fascinating techniques and crafting ideas to take your sticker art from ordinary to extraordinary. Cut stickers apart and recombine them to make brand-new designs. Distress and age them with sandpaper. Decorate them with baubles, beads and glass marbles. Coat them with lacquer to add shimmer and shine. Transform stickers with chalk, paint, glitter and more. Emboss them. Texture them. Combine stickers with fibers, tags, die cuts, wire or metal, creating fabulous and fun new elements.

When it comes to stickers and creative embellishment, the possibilities are endless!

Stickers on Stickers

Don't be afraid to cut your stickers. It won't hurt them. A pair of scissors can help you redesign and recombine your favorite sticker designs to create one-of-a kind album art. Layer stickers together to create larger scenes or provide a dimensional effect.

Santa's Little Helper

LAYER A FESTIVE SCENE

Cut, layer and overlap stickers to create a whole room full of memories. Lightly pencil angles at the bottom of the page to create room dimensions and cut paper to fit. Adhere wooden sticker planks for the floor. Overlap and layer furnishings and holiday stickers with pieces of foam tape to add dimension to the room. The chicks are eager to help, but many of their sticker accessories will have to be trimmed to a smaller scale to outfit them. Use a small piece of metallic paper for the mirror. Add letter sticker title banner, sticker-accent photos and photo captions to complete page.

Stickers Home Improvement DL, Casual Alphabet, Alphabitsy, Santa, Santa Hats, Christmas Hearth, Happy Easter, Jewel Tone DL; **Paper** Mrs. Grossman's Glacier Blue Ribbed cardstock, aqua patterned and silver metallic papers (both Paper Garden); **Other** banner die cut (Sizzix)

More Ideas

LAYER A RIVERSIDE CAMPING ADVENTURE

Stickers Meadow DL, Fir Tree, Camping

GIVE FLIGHT TO A TRANQUIL MEADOW SCENE

Stickers Studio Line Butterflies, Vellum Ferns, Twigs

Simple Pleasures
CREATE A REMINISCENT SILHOUETTE

It's easy to spread out the branches of a barren tree with the snip of the scissors. Start with a freehand-cut cardstock tree trunk. Add fullness by layering and overlapping the branch stickers with sections of leaves cut from additional branch stickers. Use circle punches to cut a tire from black cardstock; tie to the tree with natural raffia or fibers. Finish page with matted photo, journaling and letter sticker title.

Stickers Happy Haunting, Brushstroke Branches **Paper** Mrs. Grossman's Grey Day Ribbed cardstock, black cardstock; **Other** ¾" and ⅝" circle punches; natural raffia or fibers

Courtship, Love
LAYER A CONTEMPORARY BACKDROP

Make a clever, but happening, backdrop for photos and page titles with stickers and paper strips. Color-block background page with complementary-colored cardstocks with ends sliced at angles. Mat photos with vellum; mount on page. Cut vellum and metallic stickers into vertical strips and add with letter stickers to vellum panels for title and journaling pocket. Tuck a sticker accented journaling panel into pocket to complete layout.

Stickers Vellum Metallic Cool Color Blocks, Vellum Medallions, Vellum Matte Metallic DL, White Alphabet, Soft Shade Slivers DL; **Paper** sheer striped vellum, Mrs. Grossman's Mauve-elous, Just Plain Vanilla and Strawberry Shake Ribbed cardstocks and dark rose cardstock (DMD); **Other** Mrs. Grossman's Crystal Accents

Painting & Chalking Stickers

Create stunning backgrounds for your sticker art with soft washes of chalks or watercolors. Use watercolor pencils to add more detail to simple stickers. Paint alphabet letters and stickers with metallic paint or black ink to turn them into silhouettes in mere seconds.

The Amazing Race

CHALK A BREEZY STICKER BACKDROP

Hot-air-ballooning and kite-flying photos take to the sky with this quick-and-easy chalk technique. Add Design Lines stickers around pages edges. Position photos loosely on page to determine areas for chalking; do not adhere yet! See the step below to create cloud backdrop. Use a matte fixative spray to protect the chalked areas. Allow spray to dry before mounting photos. Use self-adhesive foam spacers or pieces of foam tape to layer and adhere sticker clouds and balloons and paper blocks. Complete page with blocks of journaling panels attached to page with brad fastener.

Stickers Hot Air Balloons, Clouds, Primary Slivers DL; **Paper** white, red, orange, yellow, green, blue and purple cardstock scraps; **Other** chalks; sponge-tip applicator or cotton swab; tissue for blending; self-adhesive foam tape; brad fastener

How to Add Chalk Details

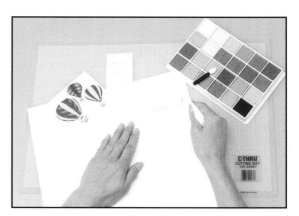

1 Lightly brush blue chalks on pages in areas where clouds, balloons and photos will be, using a sponge-tip applicator or cotton swab to blend. Blend chalk so center areas are darkest, fading chalk at outer edges. After first layer of chalk is applied, use a tissue to brush over areas to add swirl details and thicker coverage.

San Francisco

MIMIC CITY NIGHTS WITH INKED SILHOUETTES

Turn simple landmark stickers into simply sumptuous city nightlife stickers with ease. First add lavender border and Design Lines border stickers to left side of page; add more DL stickers to right side of page. Mat and mount photos. See coloring tip below to create sticker silhouettes. Mount on paper panels and frame with black paper or sticker borders for added drama. Add title, journaling block and Crystal Accents to finish. With this or any sticker-coloring technique, test ink, chalk or paint applications on sample stickers first to make sure material is colorant-friendly before starting the project.

Stickers San Francisco, Concerto DL; **Paper** violet, lavender and black cardstocks; **Other** black dye-based ink pad; silver paint pen; Mrs. Grossman's Crystal Accents

How to Create Sticker Silhouettes

1 While landmark stickers are still on the paper liner, carefully coat them with a thin layer of black ink using a stamp pad. Allow ink to dry thoroughly. Apply a second coat of ink if needed.

Gardens of Bath 1998

GIVE STICKERS TEXTURE WITH WATERCOLOR PENCIL WASH

Gentle shading on a vellum vase sticker casts a shadow of light across the journaling block. Mat photos and journaling block with pale vellum; add delicate frames constructed from Sliver Design Lines sticker borders; mount on page. Follow tips below to add texture to vase. On liner paper, add flowers behind vase and add to journaling block along with leaves and title letter stickers to finish page.

Stickers Spring Blooms, Rose Garden, Vellum Vases, Soft Shade Slivers DL; **Paper** light green and cream cardstocks, light green vellum; **Other** watercolor pencils (Staedtler); small paintbrush; water or rubbing alcohol (alcohol intensifies colors)

How to Add Watercolor Texture

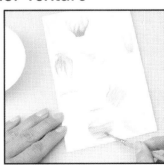

1 While still on the liner, enhance stickers with watercolor pencils by carefully shading sticker or stickers along natural shadow lines.

2 Carefully blend the penciled color with water or a tiny bit of rubbing alcohol, which dries quickly, to wash the colors and give texture to vases.

Combining Stickers With Die Cuts

Die cuts, in all shapes and sizes, introduce a new surface to decorate with stickers. Embellish precut letters or number die cuts. Use a single die-cut object as the foundation for a page element constructed from stickers. Imaginative shapes make fun, sticker-accented title and journaling panels. Design a captivating title or use a single over-sized image for impact.

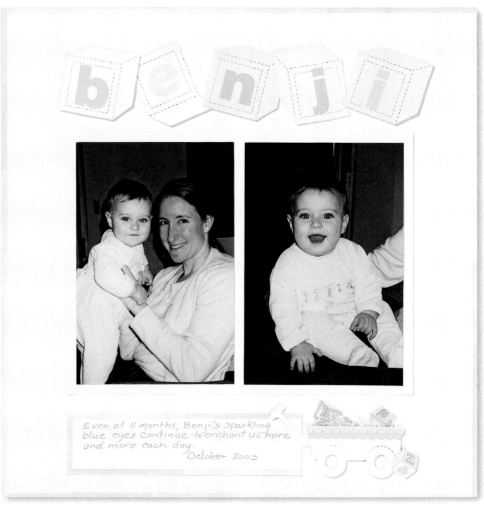

Benji

STICKER A DIE-CUT TITLE

Die cuts make a great backdrop for letter sticker titles for any page theme. First, mat photos and mount at center of page. Accent page edges with segments of Design Lines stickers. Add letter stickers to block die cuts; mount with foam spacers. Add DL accented journaling block. Finish page with sticker-accented wagon die cut filled with sticker blocks.

Stickers Vellum Alphabets, Rainbow DL, Baby Things; **Paper** Mrs. Grossman's Just Plain Vanilla, Buttered Corn, Lavender Sachet, Glacier Blue, Strawberry Shake and Celery Sticks Ribbed cardstocks; **Other** block and wagon die cuts (Sizzix)

More Ideas

FEATURE INVITING MENU ITEMS ON A TAG DIE CUT

Stickers Vegetables, Vellum Sheer Stripes DL; **Other** tag and circle set die cuts (Sizzix)

CUSTOM-COORDINATE STICKER-ACCENTED PENCIL DIE CUTS

Stickers Micro Hearts, Vellum Alphabets, Color Dots; **Other** pencil set die cuts (Sizzix)

CELEBRATE THE START OF SUMMER WITH STICKERS AND A SCHOOL BUS DIE CUT

Stickers Ext. Kids, Alphabitsy, Primary Slivers DL, Color Dots, Micro Hearts; **Other** bus die cut (Sizzix)

Sherryl and Ray

ACCENT A DIE-CUT BANNER TITLE

Appropriate for any page theme, stickers and banner die cuts go hand in hand for title ease. Mat photo, trim with Design Lines stickers and mount. Stack heart die cuts and letter and heart stickers on banner shape to create title, layering with pieces of foam tape for dimension. Finish journaling panel with DL stickers, striped metallic paper and another banner, tucking two hearts behind it.

Stickers Silver Deco Lace, Classic Alphabet, Brocade Heart, Gray Shade Slivers DL; **Paper** Mrs. Grossman's Glacier Blue and Strawberry Shake Ribbed cardstocks, silver metallic striped paper; **Other** banner and hearts set die cuts (Sizzix); Mrs. Grossman's Rose Crystal Accents

Remember This

CREATE CONTEMPORARY NUMBER DIE CUTS

Layered over number die cuts and trimmed, Design Lines stickers provide an upbeat look for any page. Mat and mount photos. Die cut shadow box numbers (both sizes) out of black cardstock. Using temporary adhesive, arrange the smaller numbers on blank sticker liner paper or wax paper. Evenly space multicolored DL stickers on the numbers. Remove from liner and trim away excess DL stickers. Mount on larger "shadow" numbers with foam tape for added dimension and adhere to page. For second part of title panel, layer colored paper strips on a black background, mat with blue cardstock and rub-on white letters. Journal on a piece of polka-dot vellum, add white rub-on lettering and attach to page using brad fasteners.

Designed by Sandi Genovese

Stickers Primary DL; **Paper** black cardstock, polka-dot vellum (Paper Adventures); **Other** shadow box number die cuts (Sizzix); white rub-on words (Making Memories); brad fasteners

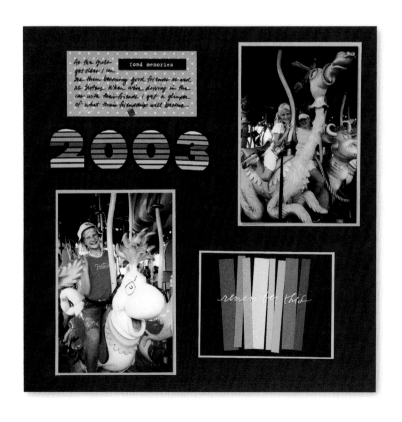

Sticker Tag Art

Big tags, little tags and every tag in between can be used for photos, journaling, titles and more. Collect an assortment of ready-made or die-cut tags so you'll have a supply on hand. Handcut several tags at a time, using a second sheet of paper to match your pages perfectly. A larger size can even be used to mat photos. Accessorize with lots of stickers, ribbons and fiber to add personality to your pages.

Friends

LINK TOGETHER ELEGANT TAGS

Use tags in all shapes and sizes to mat photos, journaling and page titles. Begin by framing page with Design Lines stickers. Mat photos with giant freehand-cut tags. Embellish with layers of foam-tape-adhered floral stickers and crystal-accented sticker bows. Cut smaller tags; adorn with title and journaling on vellum panels and connect with bow stickers. Experiment with placing two or three tags in a tight row to create a larger panel.

Stickers Bows, Wisteria, Soft Shade Slivers DL; **Paper** Mrs. Grossman's Just Plain Vanilla and Periwinkle Ribbed cardstocks and Just Plain Vanilla vellum; **Other** Mrs. Grossman's Opal Crystal Accents

More Ideas

FOCUS ON A FAVORED AND SERENE INSECT

Stickers Multi Metallic DL, OP Dragonflies, Vellum Medallions; **Other** ribbon

FEATURE A SPECIAL INITIAL OR MONOGRAM

Stickers Vellum Alphabet, Polka Dots, Stripes DL; **Other** ribbon

TRIM A PEEK-A-BOO WINDOW GIFT TAG

Stickers Vellum Medallions, Christmas Gifts, Primary Slivers DL; **Other** ribbon

LAYER GRADUATED TAGS WITH DELICATE ROSES

Stickers Vellum Pink Ribbon DL, Rosebuds; **Other** ribbon

CROP A WHIMSICAL MEDALLION TAG

Stickers OP Fairy, Wisteria; **Other** ribbon

Busy at the Playground

CREATE PLAYFUL TAG SCENES

Use tags to share the story on a playful page, decorating each one with a sticker scene. Trim page edges with Design Lines stickers. Double mat photos, hang sticker-accented tags from photos with narrow ribbon and mount on page. Build larger sticker scene on matted title and journaling block, tie with ribbons and adhere to finish page.

Stickers Playground, Chipmunks, Grass, Jewel Tone Sliver DL, Casual Alphabet; **Paper** white, yellow and red cardstocks; **Other** ¼" wide satin ribbon

Sisters

HIGHLIGHT A SPECIAL FAMILY RELATIONSHIP

Use tags and letter stickers to help feature familial ties. Mount a Design Lines sticker and paper border across upper section of page. Start this clever title by cutting seven identical-sized tags from cardstock. Center a sticker letter on each, trimming any excess overlap with scissors. Suspend tags from border with sticker tacks. Dress up additional tags with colorful sticker frames and borders. Cluster them together to hold journaling at the bottom of your page.

Stickers Vellum Medallions, Sheer Stripes DL, Twist & Torn DL, Sky Alphabet, Glitter Alphabet, Sparkle Multi Hearts, Happy Hearts, Artist Gear; **Paper** white cardstock, Royal Blue and Sky Blue cardstocks (Paper Garden)

Ribbons & Lace Stickers

Lovely lace, ribbons and fanciful notions lend a nostalgic but fresh look to layouts. Combine delicate laser-cut lace stickers with a variety of satin, grosgrain or gossamer ribbons for a touch of texture. Tie decorative bows and trims or gently weave ribbon through an entire page. Experiment with metallic threads, twine and embroidery floss for a hand-stitched effect. Use stickers for the perfect finishing touch!

Chloe

ENHANCE WOVEN RIBBON WITH STICKERS

Create a feminine showcase around page edges by combining woven ribbon and lacy stickers with a soft arch for visual appeal. Follow the steps below to create the ribbon and lace border and arch. Accent woven ribbon side borders with elegant lace stickers cut to fit border. Mat and mount photo. Add letter and lace border stickers to title blocks; mount on white cardstock and adhere. Add lace border stickers to journaling block; adhere. Use self-adhesive foam spacers or tape and cut ribbon to adhere dimensional floral sticker medallions on arch and journaling block.

Stickers White Peony, Rosebuds, Lace Edging DL, Soft Shades DL, White Alphabet; **Paper** smoke blue and ivory cardstocks; **Other** square hand punch or filmstrip punch; 1 yard of ⅜" wide white satin ribbon; self-adhesive foam tape

How to Weave a Ribbon Border

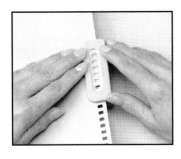

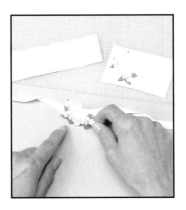

1 Punch both sides of album page with a filmstrip or square punch. Line up squares on backside of punch carefully so they are equal distances apart, repunching the last square each time for consistent spacing.

2 Weave in a 20" length of ribbon through the holes, starting from the bottom and ending with 7" of ribbon left at the top. Repeat on opposite side of page.

3 Twirl the ribbon toward the top center of the page. Use a flower sticker with self-adhesive foam spacers on the back to hold down the twirled ribbon to form arch.

4 To add flower accents to the journaling panel, cut Vs into the ends of two short pieces of ribbon. Attach them to the back of white flowers and add another flower on top using a small piece of foam spacer for depth and dimension.

How to Make a Folded Photo Card

1 Use a metal straightedge ruler and bone folder to score photo card into four equal segments, using pattern on page 108 as an example if needed, and then make the folds.

2 Use scissors and a metal ruler and craft knife to cut out photo card and make the slit at top center.

3 Select seven photos and attach one to each panel, leaving last panel blank. Use ribbon layered with Design Lines stickers to create tabs on the folding card, sandwiching 2" lengths of sticker-accented ribbons for pull-tabs.

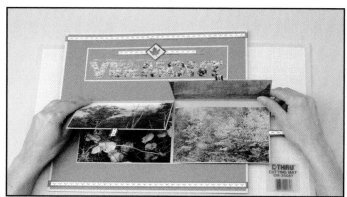

4 Mount the folded photo card on page using the blank panel to adhere. Fold to close photo card.

Vermont

UNFOLD PERFECT PICTURES WITH STICKER TABS

Pretty lace sticker tab pulls mimic page borders and serve as functional tabs for opening up a folded photo card that features seven photos in the space of just one! Die cut title letters from panoramic, duplicate or leftover photos. Place laser-cut lace borders on top of ribbon to trim page edges and title block. Trim a 12 x 12" sheet of oatmeal-colored cardstock down to 9" high by 11¾" wide or use the pattern on page 108 for trimming cardstock to size. Follow the steps above to create the folded photo card. Add journaling block to complete page.

Stickers Leaves, Henry's Lace DL, Earth Tone Page Outline; **Paper** oatmeal and terra-cotta cardstocks; **Other** ½" wide olive green grosgrain ribbon; Shadow-box alphabet die cuts (Sizzix); pattern on page 108 (optional); craft knife

Combining Stickers With Fibers

Fun, festive and fabulous fibers are an easy way to incorporate sticker art and bring texture to any page. From mesh or loosely woven fabric to tousled threads and trims, use them to embellish charms, tags, frames and panels of your photographs! Tack loose ends down with a sticker to help hold page elements in place.

Kraylyn

DANGLE FANCY-FREE STICKERS FROM FIBERS

Heart stickers take on a sweet new life, reminiscent of Valentine candies, when stuck back-to-back at fiber ends. First, trim page edges with Design Lines stickers for border. Use decorative scissors to create photo mats from buff paper and vellum; punch two holes in top of photo mat and thread fibers through back of photo mat before placing on page. Adhere back-to-back stickers on fiber ends, lightly tacking to page with a small piece of foam tape. Use paper, stickers and decorative scissors to fashion a small card that opens to reveal journaling.

Stickers Alphabitsy, Pastel Color Blocks, Glitter Beads, Sparkle Micro Hearts, Opal Patterned Hearts, Small Opal Hearts, Vellum Textile Prints DL; **Paper** Petal Pink cardstock (DMD), sheer pink vellum (Paper Adventures), buff pink paper (Paper Garden); **Other** pastel fibers (Funky Fibers); decorative scissors

More Ideas

DECORATE A SPOOKY HALLOWEEN STICKER TITLE

Stickers Spider Webs; **Other** earth-tone fibers (Funky Fibers)

TRIM A TAG WITH FREE-FORM AND EDGE STICKERS

Stickers Happy Hearts, Multi Metallic Slivers DL; **Other** pastel fibers (Funky Fibers)

STITCH A BUSY-BEE STICKER MEDALLION

Stickers African Daisy, Bees; **Other** pastel fibers (Funky Fibers)

MAKE A FURRY STICKER PANEL FIT FOR A KING

Stickers Vellum Alphabet, Lion; **Other** earth-tone fibers (Funky Fibers)

Sisters 2002

SUSPEND A METAL-RIMMED STICKER TAG FROM FIBERS

Stickers provide quick-and-easy adornment of metal-rimmed tags, perfect for any page theme. Begin by matting, layering and mounting photos on right side of page. Adhere Design Lines stickers in a crisscross shape to begin left border. Decorate circle tag with stickers and string onto a bundle of five to eight fibers. Position on front of page and fold fibers over top and bottom edges of page, threading fibers through journaling panel and attaching them securely to back of page with tape.

Stickers Vellum Medallions, Classic Alphabets; **Paper** Mrs. Grossman's Strawberry Shake and Glacier Blue Ribbed cardstocks, white vellum; **Other** metal-rimmed circle tag; pastel fibers (Funky Fibers)

Texas

ACCENT STICKER WITH TATTERED BACKGROUND

Add texture to photos and sticker art with frayed fabric. Loosen and fray the ends of mesh following the tips below. Use brown cardstock for page background. Mount frayed mesh pieces on page and mat for sticker medallion. Mount photos and sticker medallion on page and accent with barbed-wire stickers colored with black ink. Finish with letter sticker title on sticker-accented journaling block.

Stickers Texas, Mexico, Greco Columns DL; **Paper** dark brown and black cardstocks; **Other** Colormesh Origami (Aitoh Company); black ink pad

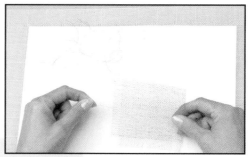

Up Close To create tattered mesh, pull and remove strings from mesh or fabric to loosen weave. Allow some of the strings to remain around the outside edges for tattered appearance.

Combining Stickers With Wire

Twist, twirl and turn paper-covered cords or wire into unique elements for your pages. Create three-dimensional artwork by mounting back-to-back stickers on the ends of wire. Substitute wire for balloon strings, flower stems and a variety of accessories when building sticker scenery. Fashion wires into imaginative titles, phrases or lettering and accent with stickers for words with pizazz.

At the Fishin' Hole

HANG PHOTOS AND STICKER ART FROM WIRE

Mimic the look of flip-down photo albums by hanging matted photos from wire with stickers. Wrap a 14" length of wire around upper page edge. Hold securely in place on back with tape. Crop and mat photos. Punch holes along the top and bottom edge of each photo panel for hanging. Accent journaling with sticker art on two or three more panels; punch holes for hanging. Carefully powder the backs of six Design Lines stickers, leaving top 1½" of each border sticky. Thread DL through photo and journaling panels, starting at bottom edge and working upwards. Loop top of DL over wire, using sticky side of border to hold in place.

Stickers Fishing, Casual Alphabet, Alphabitsy, Primary DL; **Paper** blue, yellow and white cardstocks; **Other** fine-gauge jewelry or florist's wire; ⅛" hole punch

More Ideas

HANG A PRETTY STICKER WREATH MEDALLION WITH WIRE

Stickers Holiday Decorations, Primary Slivers DL; **Other** wire

CREATE PLAYFUL MOTION WITH WIRE AND STICKERS

Stickers SP Jacks; **Other** wire

CELEBRATE A SURPRISE IN STYLE WITH STICKERS AND WIRE

Stickers OP Confetti, OP Presents; **Other** wire

Blowing Bubbles

CREATE A BUBBLY BACKDROP OF STICKERS AND WIRE

Try this great page idea for both children's and wedding photos! Freehand cut bubble bottle from metallic paper; cut out a window on bottle and tape a scrap of page protector or transparency film on the back for glass. Make a paper lid for the bottle. Position vellum stickers and journaling behind the bottle window and create a stream of vellum bubbles across page diagonally. Add letter sticker title. Twist bubble wand from wire and attach to page. Crop and mat photos with patterned paper and Design Lines stickers; mount on page.

Stickers Vellum Rainbow DL, Casual Alphabet, Vellum Bubbles; **Paper** white and light green cardstocks, lavender patterned paper, light green metallic paper (Paper Garden); **Other** page protector or transparency film; light green wire

Groovy Garb

FASHION STYLIN' SHADES WITH STICKERS AND WIRE

Add this fashion statement to any retro page that calls for coolness! Start with a color-blocked background accented with Design Lines stickers. Add sticker-accented photos. Cut and twist wire to form eyeglass frames. Fill in lens with large vellum bubble stickers. Complete page with colorful letter sticker title and journaling.

Stickers Primary Bubbles, Glitter Alphabet, Glitter Beads, Primary Slivers DL, Jewel Tone Slivers DL; **Paper** yellow, red, blue and lime green cardstock scraps, white cardstock; **Other** fine-gauge jewelry or florist's wire

Accenting Stickers With Jewels
Combine tiny crystals, beads and jewels with stickers to create glimmering works of art on your pages. Adhere gems directly to a page or combine with metallic threads or even pieces of chain for unique borders and sticker accents.

A Pirate's Life for Me
SHOWCASE A BEJEWELED TREASURE TROVE

Create a sticker and jewel cache that any pirate would be proud of! First, add red Design Lines stickers around page to create border. Mat photo and journaling block. Add Crystal Accents and mount. Sprinkle Crystal Accents and beads across matted letter sticker title and lower page corners.

Stickers Parrots, Sparkle Treasure Chest, Vellum Alphabet; **Paper** red and black cardstocks; **Other** Mrs. Grossman's Clear Crystal Accents; multicolor faux jewels and beads

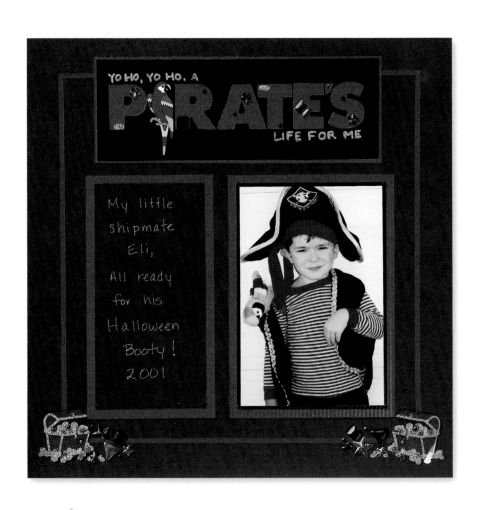

More Ideas

TRIM A DIMENSIONAL TREE

Stickers Reflections Tree, White Alphabet, Holly DL, Classic Page Outline; **Other** Mrs. Grossman's Ruby and Topaz Crystal Accents

DRESS UP A DANCING HORSE

Stickers Circus, Vellum Pink Ribbon DL; **Other** Mrs. Grossman's Multi-Color Crystal Accents

ENHANCE AN ELEGANT WREATH

Stickers Vellum Pastel Color Blocks, Heart Wreath; **Other** Mrs. Grossman's Opal Crystal Accents

And the Stockings Were Hung

DECK THE HALLS WITH JEWELED STICKERS

Layered pine bough and sticker stockings glow with charm when accented with Crystal Accents. Cut pine bough stickers and layer across top of page, placing small pieces of foam tape between each layer for dimension. Top the border with a Chickadee sticker and Crystal Accents. Hang bejeweled stockings using foam tape for depth. Double mat photo, add letter sticker title, journaling block and some additional crystals; mount all on page to complete.

Stickers Chickadee, RF Stockings, Classic Alphabets; **Paper** oatmeal, chili and evergreen cardstocks; **Other** Mrs. Grossman's Emerald, Ruby, Topaz and Opal Crystal Accents

A Kiss From Kazzy

GIVE ANIMAL STICKERS THE ROYAL TREATMENT

Camel stickers leap to life with embroidery thread and jewel harnesses for a perfect page accent for uncommon photos. Layer paper at bottom of page to form sand dunes, inserting palm tree stickers at different heights between each layer. Cut tent tops from stickers and build desert tents using paper and vellum. Attach camel caravan to page using small pieces of foam tape. Loop thread or twine across camels, tucking ends behind stickers. Apply Crystal Accents to thread, camels and at the top of each tent. Finish with letter sticker title and sticker-accented photos.

Stickers Carnival Rides, Purple and Red Stickers By the Yard, Casual Alphabet, PW Palm Tree, Camels; **Paper** Mrs. Grossman's Atmosphere ribbed cardstock, sand-textured paper, white cardstock and vellum; **Other** Mrs. Grossman's Multi-Color Crystal Accents; silver twine or thread

Accenting Stickers With Glass Marbles

Make your sticker art shimmer, sparkle and shine with grainy texture! Tiny glass marbles can easily be applied to the surface of stickers using a thin layer of glue or adhesive. The best effects are achieved when beads are applied to pale or metallic finishes such as silver, gold or white. Apply beads while stickers are still on the liner paper so excess can be gently shaken off or removed. Use a bead tray to corral any loose marbles with ease.

Celebrate the Wonder of the Season

ADD TEXTURE WITH TINY GLASS MARBLES

Bring shiny glitz to stickers with adhesive and tiny glass marbles. Follow the steps below to create the jingle bells. Journal on vellum panels and fill title with a thin layer of adhesive and micro beads or fine grain glitter. When photos and sticker ribbon borders are in place on page, attach jingle bells and journaling.

Stickers Christmas Ribbons DL, Jingle Bells; **Paper** white and oatmeal cardstocks; **Other** clear tiny glass marbles (Halcraft); double-sided adhesive tape or sheet adhesive

How to Apply Tiny Glass Marbles

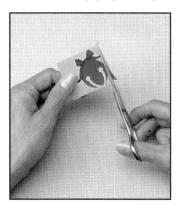

1 Cover the stickers with double-sided tape or sheet adhesive. Cut out the shape of the sticker.

2 Peel back the tape liner, exposing sticky part of tape on surface of sticker.

3 Place the sticker face down in container of tiny glass marbles. Press beads firmly into adhesive with fingers or roll with a brayer to coat the sticker with plenty of the glass marbles.

4 Once the sticker is coated, trim a bow from another sticker and place on top of the glass marbles for a dimensional look.

Boys and Their Toys

MAKE CHILD'S PLAY OF HARD LABOR

Use tiny glass marbles to add texture to scenic sticker medallions. Begin by adhering a Design Lines sticker across lower border of page. Build sticker scenes on medallions of matted cardstock, trimming any excess overlap from stickers. Embellish each scene by building mounds of "dirt" out of tiny glass marbles. Mat and mount photos. Create letter sticker title in same fashion as border medallions. Add matted journaling to complete layout.

Stickers Chipmunks, Home Improvement DL, Construction Equipment, Casual and Spice Vellum Alphabets; **Paper** brown and oatmeal cardstocks; **Other** gold tiny glass marbles (Halcraft)

We Do Not Remember Days

FOCUS ATTENTION ON STICKER DETAIL

Isolate and accent specific portions of stickers with tiny glass marbles to create the illusion of motion and depth. See the tips below to create lower sticker border accent. Double mat photo and mount on page. Add accent stickers, journaling and letter sticker title to finish page.

Stickers Classic Alphabet, Ocean DL, Gray Shades DL; **Paper** black, white and sand cardstocks; **Other** gold and clear tiny glass marbles (Halcraft)

Up Close

To accent with tiny glass marbles, place marbles on a small precise area of a sticker using a glue pen. Press tiny marbles into the layer of glue and gently remove any excess. Work inside a tray or shoe-box lid so excess marbles can easily be returned to the original container.

Accenting Stickers With Glitter

Shake up your sticker art with a sprinkle of glitter. Glamorize white, laser-cut or matte-finish designs with a veiling of iridescent or pearl glitter. Use a thin line of glue and loose glitter to title a page or journaling panel with glistening script. A little glitter goes a long way so apply glitter to stickers while they are still on the liner paper rather than on your album page. Accent stickers with glitter to call attention to detail with glitz!

Fairy

ADD A WISP OF FAIRY DUST TO STICKERS

Just a hint of glitter is all it takes to dress up stickers with an ever-so-subtle touch. Apply glitter to Wisteria stickers while they are still on the liner paper. Position sticker art on layered green vellum title and journaling mats. Once page is complete, use glue stick to create a subtle "flight path" beneath fairy sticker and lightly dust with glitter. Apply letter sticker title and finish with journaling and mounting photos.

Stickers OP Fairies, Classic Alphabet, Wisteria; **Paper** Mrs. Grossman's Sage Advice Ribbed cardstock, pale green and green vellums; **Other** fine-grain glitter; glue; small brush

More Ideas

STRING A SEASONAL GREETING
Stickers Merry Christmas, Christmas Lights, Primary Slivers DL

SWEETLY ENHANCE CELESTIAL BODIES
Stickers OP Sun, Moon and Stars; **Other** ribbon

MAKE WEDDING BELLS SHINE
Stickers Silver Deco Lace DL, Wedding Bell; **Other** Mrs. Grossman's Opal Crystal Accents

Winter

SPRINKLE SOME GLISTENING STICKER SNOWFLAKES

Frame a page with silver Design Lines stickers and glitter-accented snowflake stickers to feature chilly photos. Frame the page with multiple silver DL stickers. While snowflakes are still on the liner paper, apply a thin layer of glue, sprinkle with glitter and let dry. For a more colorful effect, try lightly chalking the snowflakes in shades of lavender and ice blue before adding glitter. Tear edges of vellum to mat photos and snowflake medallion; mount. Finish layout with letter sticker title and journaling.

Stickers PW Snowflakes, Metallic Slivers DL, Classic Alphabet; **Paper** navy blue cardstock, white vellum; **Other** fine-grain glitter; glue or glue pen

Making Cookies

BAKE SOME SUGARY SWEET STICKER COOKIES

Whip up some good-enough-to-eat treats using stickers and glitter. Begin with color-blocked background accented with a Design Lines sticker. Cut a cookie sheet from silver paper. Write title with a glue pen; add loose glitter without smearing writing. Use glue pen and sprinkle cookie stickers with glitter. When cookie sheet is dry, attach cookies using small pieces of foam tape. Use a few additional cookies and cooking stickers to highlight recipe used as journaling panel. Finish with letter sticker photo captions.

Stickers Christmas Cookies, Twilight and Ruby Stickers By the Yard, Soft Shade Slivers DL, Cooking Equipment, Alphabitsy; **Paper** cream and tan cardstocks, cream vellum, silver metallic paper (Paper Garden); **Other** glitter; glue pen

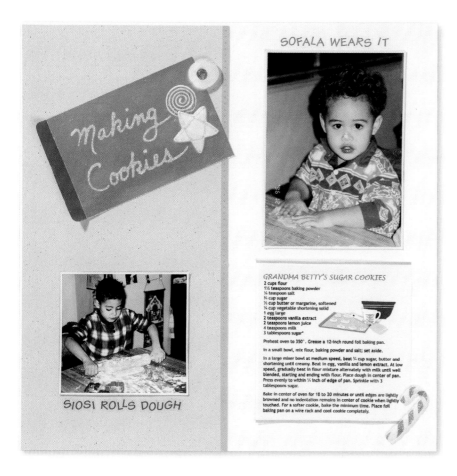

Accenting Stickers With Lacquer & Glass Pebbles

Add clear luster and shine to sticker art with lacquers and glass. Coating titles or specific stickers with a clear glaze easily adds definition or dimension to a page. While coating is still wet, sprinkle with iridescent or multicolored glitter for a touch of sparkle. Make sure that lacquered area is completely dry before transferring stickers to page. Attach a glass pebble on top of a sticker to magnify a section of your artwork. Glass can also be used to create the illusion of water droplets.

Catch of the Day

LAND A WET STICKER FISH WITH LACQUER

A generous layer of clear crystal lacquer along with a sprinkle of glitter gives stickers a slick finish. Begin with Design Lines stickers around page edges. Crop, mat and mount photos. Extend fishing pole from photo to page with a sticker pole segment. Add lacquer and glitter to fish sticker while still on liner paper; once dry, mount on page with foam tape, positioning sticker near photograph so it appears to have jumped out onto the page. Complete page with letter sticker title, water splash stickers and framed journaling block.

Stickers Studio Line Fish, Jewel Tones DL, Jewel Tone Slivers DL, Vellum Alphabets, Splash, Alphabitsy, Camping; **Paper** Mrs. Grossman's Glacier Blue Ribbed cardstock, white cardstock

More Ideas

USE LACQUER AND GLITTER TO ANIMATE STICKERS

Stickers Heart Throb, Flutterbugs, Clouds

MANUFACTURE PLASTIC BUTTONS WITH LACQUER ON STICKERS

Stickers Lace Edging DL, Buttons, Lace Medallions; **Other** ribbon

GIVE CANDLE STICKERS A WAXY QUALITY

Stickers Candles, Vellum Medallions, Easter DL, Party Greetings; **Other** ribbon

COAT A STICKER BOUQUET WITH DEWY FRESHNESS

Stickers Wedding Accessories, Soft Shade Sliver DL

Water Works

MAGNIFY WATER SPLASHES WITH PEBBLES

Use clear page pebbles anytime you want to exaggerate a sticker accent. Trim background page with Design Lines stickers around all edges. Tear a blue border. Mat photos and journaling block; mount. Create letter sticker title and accent with water splash stickers. Make a spray of water splashes; cover some splashes with page pebbles to magnify.

Stickers Water DL, Aqua Vellum Alphabet, Primary Slivers DL; **Paper** white and bright blue cardstocks; **Other** clear glass pebbles; clear crystal lacquer (Sakura Hobby Craft)

Heather

SPLASH STICKER TILES WITH LACQUER

Create a slippery wet bathtub scene with stickers and clear crystal lacquer. First, trim page edges with Design Lines stickers. Mount photo. Coat vellum color blocks and bathtub stickers with a thin layer of lacquer while stickers are still on the liner paper. Sprinkle glitter onto the bathtub suds and soap. When lacquer is completely dry, create bath scene on paper panel, starting with color tiles first. Add duck using a small piece of foam tape to attach character to page. Position bathtub in front of duck to create the illusion that it is in water, using more foam tape for dimension. Add letter sticker title, journaling, mat and mount on page.

Stickers Bathtub, Baby's First Toys, Vellum Color Blocks, Vellum Rainbow DL, Alphabitsy; **Paper** white and pink cardstocks, pink vellum; **Other** fine-grain glitter; clear crystal lacquer (Sakura Hobby Craft); foam tape

Sunflowers

VIEW FLOWERS THROUGH A "GLASS" WINDOW

Square page pebbles make excellent "glass" for sticker windows. Mat yellow trimmed background with blue cardstock. To create window, cut a 3" square of blue paper and trim to fit inside window frame. Position sunflower blossom in center of square and top with window sticker. Place one square pebble inside each windowpane. Construct journaling panel and "pop" a potted sunflower on right edge. Trim a black sticker border to resemble handle and make bee's magnifying glass using ladybug sticker and a round page pebble. Complete the layout with sticker-accented photos and letter sticker title.

Stickers Sunflower, PW Window, Casual Alphabet, Garden Tools, Bees, Ladybugs, Jewel Tone Slivers DL, Basic Black & White DL; **Paper** yellow and royal blue cardstocks; **Other** round and square page pebbles

Stickers & Embossing

A staple for rubber stamp artists, embossing powder also adds dimensional detail to your favorite stickers. Make sure to test the powder on a sample to determine the amount of powder and drying time needed before proceeding on your scrapbook artwork. You will notice that vellum and more porous types of sticker surfaces work the best. To use embossing powder on glossy stickers, gently rub surface with fine-grain sandpaper before applying powder. Experiment with dry embossing by passing stickers through a paper crimper or tracing them with embossing templates or stencils to create interesting raised patterns.

Water Lilies

ADD SUN-KISSED TEXTURE WITH EMBOSSING POWDER

Accenting just a little of a sticker's outline can add to its subtle and serene detail without stealing attention from photos. Mat photos and letter sticker title with vellum. Tear top edge of large section of blue vellum to create pond at bottom of page; add water lily stickers and journaling. Carefully etch detail onto edges and petals of each flower with an embossing pen; sprinkle with embossing powder and set with heat gun until area appears raised. Add journaling to finish page.

Stickers Vellum Water Lilies, Vellum Alphabets; **Paper** pink cardstock, blue vellum; **Other** embossing powder and pen; heat-embossing gun

Nobody "Nose" Fun Like a Clown

CAUSE A COMMOTION WITH CRIMPED GEOMETRICS

Simple embossed geometric stickers add a playful and colorful backdrop for a fun photo such as this. While letter stickers are still on the liner paper, tint letters blue with an ink pad. Run geometric stickers through crimper to create a wavy, embossed texture across each shape. Add photo and trim with Design Lines stickers.

Stickers PW Alphabet, Ext. Geometrics, Alphabitsy; **Paper** white cardstock; **Other** Deco Color Opaque Paint Marker in blue (Marvy Uchida); Wave Lil' Boss paper crimper (Paper Adventures)

Distressing Stickers

Designed to hold their colors and quality on your album pages for 50 years or more, stickers, paper and metals can be "aged" by rubbing them with sandpaper to create a textured, vintage or whitewashed finish. Crinkle, crease or wad stickers and then flatten to create the look of rustic metal or antique fabric.

September 11, 2001

CRUMPLE STICKERS FOR A GALVANIZED LOOK

Distressed stickers can capture an emotional moment in time, letting the photos tell the story. Carefully wrinkle Design Lines and metallic vellum square stickers while on the liner paper. Remove from liner and place them on page. Crop and mount photos. Journal on panels torn from same paper used for page; mount using small pieces of foam tape. Attach heart pin on page.

Stickers Gray Shade Slivers DL, Silver Deco Lace DL, Metallic Vellum Color Blocks; **Paper** Cement cardstock (Paper Garden), silver metallic paper; **Other** red heart pin (Mrs. Grossman's)

Our Little Sweetheart

DISTRESS STICKERS FOR SOFT APPEAL

Combine a brushed-metal frame with distressed stickers for cool sweetness. Cut window frame from metal, gently bending back center section to create shutters. Rub metal's surface vigorously with sandpaper to create look of brushed metal. While stickers are still on the liner paper, rub them with sandpaper to create a grainy, worn look. Accent metal frame around stickers with a piercing tool or nail. Assemble page by adding matted photo, aged letter sticker title and journaling.

Stickers Red Heart, Vellum Alphabet, Basic Red & White DL; **Paper** black, white and red cardstocks; **Other** thin sheets of aluminum (Making Memories); fine-grain sandpaper

Accenting Moving Pictures With Stickers

Sometimes one picture is just not enough! Share the whole story behind the page by building moving elements or pullout photo panels. Start sequencing photos while the film is still in the camera. Capture candid moments between two relatives during the big event. Take photos of your child dressing for the big game or warming the bench in addition to the action shots. Include signs, plaques or landmarks for more memorable vacation photos—and let stickers help tell your photojournalistic story!

Emily's Many Faces

SPIN A STICKER-ACCENTED PHOTO SHOWCASE

Use framing Design Lines stickers, letter stickers and photos to spin a photo tale with ease. Follow the steps below to create the spinning photo wheel. Frame backside edges of pink cardstock with self-adhesive foam tape; mount overlay on top of circle background, aligning left-hand edges. Decorate front of pink cardstock overlay with sticker borders and alphabet letters cut from fabric sticker sheets to complete page.

Stickers Spring Linen Fabric Sheet and DL, Classic Alphabet, Metallic Sliver DL, Spring Linen Pink Ribbon DL; **Paper** Mrs. Grossman's Strawberry Shake and Glacier Blue Ribbed cardstocks, white cardstock; **Other** compass or 10" dinner plate; decorative scissors; brad fastener

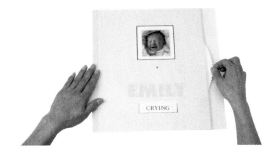

How to Make a Spinning Photo Wheel

1 Use a compass or a dinner plate to trace a 10" diameter circle onto white cardstock; cut out. Trim outside edge of circle with decorative scissors. Layer circle atop background page, center, and punch a 1/8" hole in center through both layers.

2 Trim pink cardstock overlay to 12 x 10½". Cut a 3½" square out of center of pink paper, 1½" down from top edge, for photo viewing window. Cut a 1 x 3½" rectangle out of center of paper, 1½" above bottom edge, for letter sticker journaling window. Accent both windows with silver Design Lines stickers.

3 Crop three photos to 2¾" squares. Spin paper wheel and position and attach each photo to wheel so that it is centered in window. Once photos are placed, spin wheel again to place titles in lower window. Attach circle to blue background page using brad fastener through punched holes. Layer pink page over wheel and blue page, matching edges. Connect all three layers with brad fastener and secure edges.

My First Haircut

FEATURE BEFORE AND AFTER PHOTOS WITH STICKERS

A sliding strip of pictures and sticker captions captures each expression before, during and after a milestone event. Begin by cutting a 3½" square out of right edge of background cardstock. Cut a 1½ x 3½" rectangle 2" above the square to hold sticker captions. Trim aqua cardstock to a 9 x 12" panel. Crop photos to 4" squares and tile across panel. Position titles 2 inches above each photo. Using pieces of foam tape, build two channels on back of album page 1½" from top and bottom edges. Place two or three small foam tape stops on the left edge of aqua panel to prevent it from sliding out. Position the aqua panel with photos and stickers on it between the two foam-tape channels on back of page; cover with a scrap sheet of trimmed 12 x 12" cardstock to hold in place. Mat and mount photo and journaling block. Trim page, window openings and all mats with Design Lines stickers. Hang sticker charms on ribbon for letter sticker title panel. Finish with a sticker pull-tab on right-hand edge of photo slide. Slit side of page protector so panel can be pulled out and viewed.

Stickers Hair Cut, Primary DL, Primary Sliver DL, Casual Alphabet, White Alphabet;
Paper Mrs. Grossman's Glacier Blue Ribbed cardstock, yellow and blue cardstocks;
Other ¼" wide satin ribbon

This is a Problem

DOCUMENT A PHOTO SERIES WITH STICKERS AND JOURNALING

The story of a stolen ball unfolds across five panels of pictures, delighting both readers and dog when the two are reunited. A narrative accented with stickers is written on the back. First, accent page edges with Design Lines stickers. To create the story panel, cut four panels of cardstock to 4 x 6". Hinge panels together with pieces of tape. You now have eight panels, counting the front and back, on which to mount photos, journaling and sticker art. Mount five photos on panels, reserving back of last panel to attach your foldout story to page. Add journaling and sticker scene to remaining two panels. Create tennis ball pull-tab by punching circle out of lime paper and adding white pen-stroke seams. Complete layout with matted blurb sticker mounted with foam spacers and letter sticker title.

Stickers Concerto DL, Blurb, Alphabitsy, Neighborhood Dogs, Puppies; **Paper** oatmeal cardstock (Paper Garden), lime cardstock; **Other** white paint pen; ½" circle punch

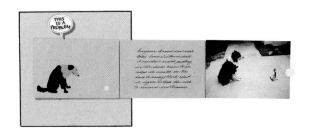

Stickers & Metal

Whether it's specialty paper or thin sheets of actual embossing metals, it's easy to create your own lustrous page accents out of metal. Combine metal with stickers. Or, add a gilded touch to stickers with a silver paint pen or a dab of metallic pigment paint for an embellishment technique that won't scratch or harm your photographs. Use faux metal stickers for weathered finishes and metalwork made easy!

A Boy and His Dog

ACCENT EMBOSSED METAL WITH SILHOUETTED STICKERS

Silhouetting stickers (see page 75) is a nice way to create simple sticker accents over metal, allowing the focus of a page to remain on photos. To ink stickers that have a glossy finish, lightly sand them first. While stickers are still on paper liner, paint stickers with black ink pad. A second coat may be necessary. Allow drying time before handling or using on page. Follow the steps below to create the embossed metal dog bone. Create four panels to form embossed metal journaling frame in the same manner. Flip each metal piece over before attaching to the page to showcase the full effect of the embossed metal. Assemble metallic page borders, photos, metal and sticker art and mount on page. Finish with metal-framed sticker journaling block.

Stickers Grass, Ext. Kids, Giant Dogs, PW Alphabet, Concerto DL; **Paper** black cardstock, silver metallic paper (Paper Garden), white pinstripe vellum (Making Memories); **Other** pattern on page 109; aluminum sheet (Making Memories); black ink pad; embossing stylus or nail; scrap foam core board or mouse pad

How to Pierce Metal

1 Size and photocopy bone pattern on page 109; cut out. Lightly trace bone shape onto metal sheet using the fine-point tip of an embossing stylus.

2 Use scissors to cut out embossed metal bone.

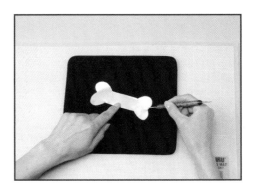

3 Put metal bone on scrap foam core board or mouse pad and gently emboss small holes around the outside edge of bone using an embossing stylus. If desired, you can pierce the metal holes instead of embossing by piercing the metal all the way through with a piercing tool or a nail.

Chino Aircraft Museum

USE STICKERS WITH METAL TO TELL A RIVETING STORY

A metal title and brads, along with stickers and photos, help fasten one's attention on this interesting aircraft page. Die cut letters from aluminum sheet. Use a small nail or piercing tool to dry emboss small holes on three to four outside corners of each letter, being careful not to pierce all the way through the metal. This will make it look like rivets are holding letters to page. Adhere letters to page, building sticker art around them to create title. Create an illusion of motion on page by trimming tail portion off plane, aligning cut edge with page edge. Crop photos; mat with vellum and Design Lines stickers and mount on page. Finish with small metal brads for rivets and add journaling.

Stickers Vintage Aircraft, Jewel Tone Slivers DL, Classic Alphabet; **Paper** gray and charcoal cardstocks, gray pinstripe vellum (Making Memories); **Other** aluminum sheet (Making Memories); Shadow box alphabet dies (Sizzix); ¼" silver brad fasteners; nail or piercing tool

Maine

COMBINE AGED STICKERS AND METAL MESH

Trap some crusty sticker crustaceans in metal cages to help highlight seaside village fishing photos. Mat photos with cardstock, accent with scrap metal block stickers, layer and mount on page. Rub lobster stickers with sandpaper to distress. Cut cage frames from metal sticker sheet and border edges with gold Design Line stickers. Place frames on top of mesh, loosening weave of fabric if needed. Position lobsters on page and mount cages on top. Finish with metal letter sticker title, matted journaling block and lobster sticker medallion.

Stickers Lobster, Scrap Metal Alphabet, Blocks and Full Sheets, Metallic Slivers DL; **Paper** terra-cotta and black cardstocks; **Other** gold metallic mesh; fine-grain sandpaper; gold paint pen

Sticker Art Showcase

Now that you've seen all of the fun and unique ways to use stickers to help tell your photo stories on scrapbook pages, we just had to show you a few more amazing sticker-art scrapbook pages to inspire you. Enjoy!

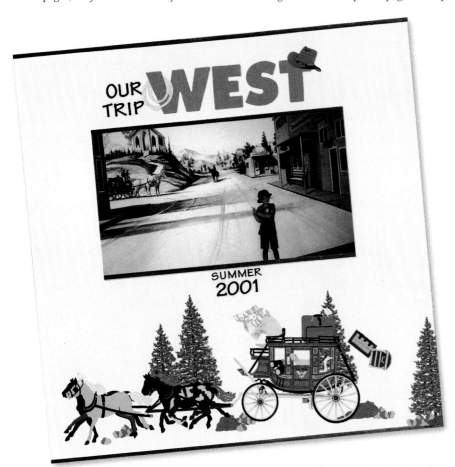

Our Trip West

Build sticker scenery across bottom of page. Accent title with a few more stickers. Border top and bottom edges of page and photo.

Stickers Earth Tone Page Outlines, Stagecoach, Giant Luggage, Fir Tree, Construction Equipment, Home Improvement DL, Small Farm Animals; **Paper** cream and green cardstocks

Bob the Builder

Tile page caption across bottom edge using layered panels of paper and stickers. Use pumpkin stickers to accent title and journaling while adding to the orange and yellow color scheme.

Stickers Small Jack-O-Lanterns, Halloween DL; **Paper** black, orange and yellow cardstocks

Go Giants

Die cut letters and accent with stickers and shadow die cuts. Construct baseball field from cardstock as page background.

Stickers Baseball, Sports; **Paper** orange, green, brown and white cardstocks; **Other** shadow-letter die cuts (Sizzix)

Santa's Holly-Day Helper

Fill a wagon die-cut with photographic stickers to mirror photo. Layer green, red and cream cardstocks for elegant photo mats and journaling panels.

Stickers Classic Alphabet, Christmas Gifts, Holly Sprigs; **Paper** dark green, cream and red cardstocks; **Other** wagon die cut (Sizzix)

Searching for Seashells

Layer shell stickers with vellum letter stickers and beach torn from paper to create a soft beach scene.

Stickers Vellum Alphabets, Seashells; **Paper** Mrs. Grossman's Atmosphere Ribbed cardstock, sand cardstock

Emily

Create soft and serene mats and borders from delicate blue vellum and lace stickers. Stack baby carriages with foam tape and gently coat top sticker with iridescent glitter. Weave vellum Design Lines sticker through carriage, like ribbon.

Stickers Blue Linen Ribbon DL, Baby Carriage, Vellum Medallions, Rainbow DL, Classic Alphabet; **Paper** Mrs. Grossman's Lavender Sachet Ribbed cardstock and periwinkle vellum; **Other** foam tape; glue stick or pen; fine-grain glitter

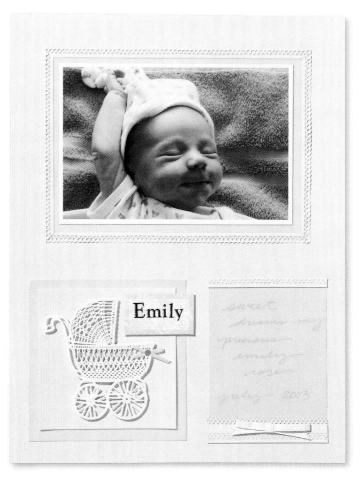

Caution: Wild Animals

Use a die-cut sign and a handcut tree stump shape to hold journaling. The tree stump is hinged on the left-hand edge and opens to reveal journaling. Accent your paper panels with delicate vellum ferns and watercolor stickers.

Stickers Studio Line Baby Animals, Songbirds, Wild Flowers, Vellum Ferns, Alphabitsy, Jewel Tone Slivers DL; **Paper** tan, light green and light brown textured cardstocks; **Other** sign die cut (Sizzix); brown colored pencil

Tea Garden

Build a color-blocked tile border around a page using vellum stickers. Select only yellow and green tones to keep an analogous color scheme. Cut sections of fern stickers and layer on top of larger squares to add a botanical theme to the mosaic. Use tiny squares or blocks as corner accents on panels.

Stickers Vellum Pastel Color Blocks, Rainbow DL, Celery Alphabet, Vases, Branches, Ferns; **Paper** White Linen paper (Paper Garden)

Sunset

Use solid colors with simple black stickers to highlight a dramatic photograph.

Stickers Abigail Caps, Brushstrokes Marsh Life; **Paper** azure blue and yellow cardstocks

Rome, Italy

Layer three Coliseum stickers with foam tape to create a dimensional structure. Frame inside edges of paper panels with sections cut from trees and clouds. Mat each panel and entire page with black paper to add definition.

Stickers Abigail Caps, Oak Tree, Clouds, Rome, Park; **Paper** Mrs. Grossman's Periwinkle and Twilight Ribbed cardstocks, black and goldenrod cardstocks

Santa Barbara

Build an ornate paper and sticker window and mount on your page with foam tape to create a dimensional pocket for journaling.

Stickers Wrought Iron Fence DL, PW Palm Trees, Jewel Tone Slivers DL, Soft Shade Slivers DL; **Paper** tan, dark brown, light blue and rust cardstocks, cream vellum, cream parchment

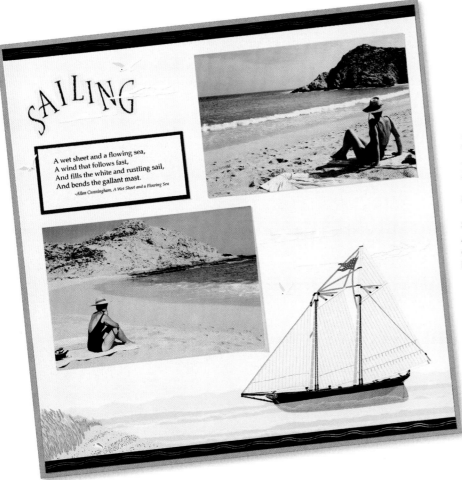

Sailing

Place the sailboat in layers of vellum water and build a sticker beach around it. Using large-sized stickers can create impact on a page.

Stickers Abigail Caps, Ocean DL, Vellum Water DL, America, Celebrate Stickers By the Yard; **Paper** tan, cream and black cardstocks, Mrs. Grossman's Glacier Blue Ribbed cardstock

Page Title Showcase

Here are more inspirational ideas for incorporating stickers into your page titles. Simply locate an idea that appeals to you, and use the basic idea to create a similar page title for any page theme by altering the papers and stickers that you use. It's that easy!

Nature Hike

Cut tag from cardstock. Tile metal block stickers across center and bottom edge of tag. Color letters in with black ink to create title. Pop watercolor stickers at bottom edge.

Stickers Scrap Metal Blocks, White Alphabet, Studio Line Butterflies, Studio Line Wildflowers; **Paper** tan and black cardstocks; **Other** 3/8" wide organza ribbon; black ink pad

Our Sweet Baby

Decorate pink tags with stickers and pop across layered paper panels.

Stickers Pink Calico Full Sheet, Baby Things, Classic Alphabet; **Paper** pink and lavender cardstocks

My Love Bug

Layer cardstock panels at bottom of vellum tag. Build sticker scene, layering foam tape behind top tier of grass. Reinforce hole at top of tag with folded Design Lines stickers.

Stickers Heart Throb, Vellum Polka Dots & Stripes DL, Love Bugs, Flutterbugs, African Daisy, Grass, Casual Alphabet; **Paper** pink vellum, white and red cardstocks; **Other** 1/8" wide grosgrain ribbon

Love

Stack stickers on medallions of black paper. Tile title across silver paper, adhering each panel with foam tape. Frame with pink Design Lines stickers.

Stickers Wedding Bell, Scrap Metal Alphabet, Soft Shade Slivers DL; **Paper** black cardstock, silver metallic paper; **Other** 1½" square punch

Easter

Punch letters out of blocks of cardstock and build elaborate sticker scenes on vellum to back the outline left in each panel. Animate Easter chicks with foam tape. You'll even end up with an extra set of lavender letters to use elsewhere!

Stickers Ext. Happy Easter, Vellum Grass DL, Clouds; **Paper** Mrs. Grossman's Lavender Sachet and Periwinkle Ribbed cardstocks, lime cardstock, blue vellum

Birthday

Decorate letters with colorful sticker bits and pieces. Dance title across layered paper panels and frame with multiple Design Lines stickers.

Stickers Easter DL, Vellum Alphabet Letters, Ext. Happy Easter; **Paper** Mrs. Grossman's Strawberry Shake Ribbed cardstock, lavender cardstock

Baby Boy

Quilt and crop fabric stickers to create a fabulous title panel.

Stickers French Country Fabric Panels and Sheets, Baby Boy; **Paper** light blue cardstock

Paris

Layer stickers with foam tape and paper panels to create a festive title scene.

Stickers Fireworks, Paris, Classic Alphabet; **Paper** red and black cardstocks

New Home

Ink alphabet letters to turn them black. Place fabric swatches on panels of cardstock and layer with foam tape to create a whimsical title to accessorize a page.

Stickers Basic Black Fabrics Full Sheet and Swatches, Vellum Alphabets; **Paper** red and white cardstocks; **Other** black ink pad

Our Vacation to Hawaii

Dress up basic cardstock with layered vellum borders, Hawaiian stickers and a title stacked with foam tape.

Stickers Fabric Hawaiian Shirts, Fabric Beach Gear, PW Palm Trees, Hawaii, Vellum Sheer Stripes DL, Vellum Ribbon DL, Vellum Alphabet, Alphabitsy; **Paper** dark green and white cardstocks

Trick or Treat

Create your own lettering style with Halloween candy stickers. Outline letters with a black pen so they really stand out against layers of yellow, orange and black cardstocks.

Stickers Halloween Candy, Casual Alphabet, Alphabitsy; **Paper** orange, yellow and black cardstocks

Go Bears

Decorate die-cut letters and paper panels with a medley of blue borders, basketballs and bears, using foam tape to add dimension behind each element.

Stickers Grizzly Bear, Basketball, Basic Navy & White DL, Primary Slivers DL; **Paper** yellow and blue cardstocks

Patterns

Use these helpful patterns to complete scrapbook pages featured in this book. Enlarge a pattern by the percentage shown and photocopy the pattern. When transferring patterns to your paper of choice, be sure to note solid, continuous lines for cut lines and dotted lines for fold lines.

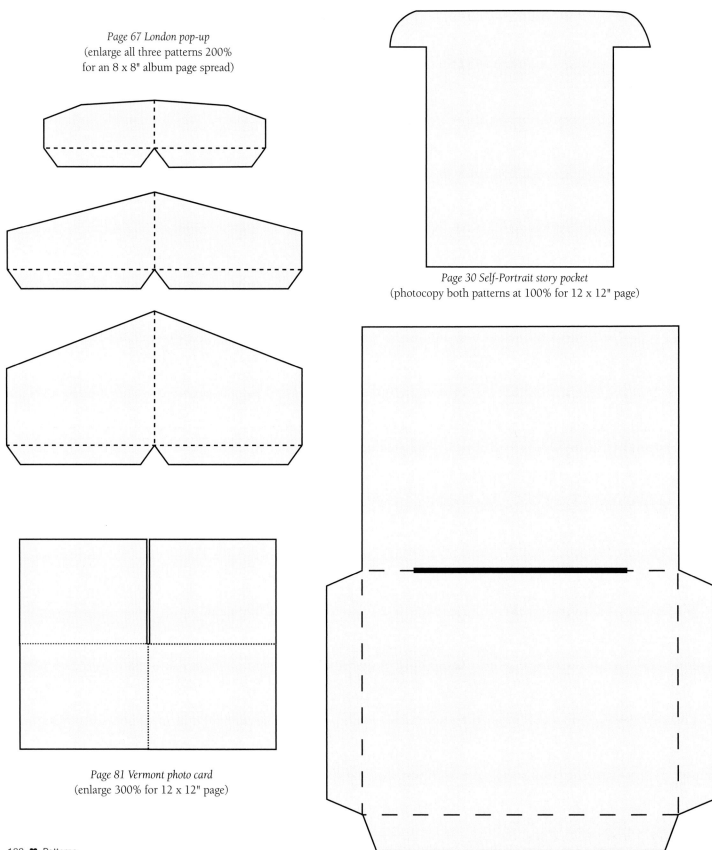

Page 67 London pop-up
(enlarge all three patterns 200%
for an 8 x 8" album page spread)

Page 30 Self-Portrait story pocket
(photocopy both patterns at 100% for 12 x 12" page)

Page 81 Vermont photo card
(enlarge 300% for 12 x 12" page)

Page 66 Splash spiral pop-up
(photocopy pattern at 100%
for an 8 x 8" album page spread)

Page 49 Spring Grasses weaving
(enlarge 200% for an 8 x 8" page)

Page 98 A Boy and His Dog bone
(enlarge 200% for 12 x 12" page)

Page 31 Cotswolds window
(photocopy pattern at 100% for 12 x 12" page)

Sources

The following companies manufacture products featured in this book. Please check your local retailers to find these materials. In addition, we have made every attempt to properly credit the items mentioned in this book. We apologize to any company that we have listed incorrectly or if the sources were unknown, and we would appreciate hearing from you.

3m®
(800) 364-3577
www.3m.com

Aitoh Company
(800) 681-5533
www.aitoh.com

All Night Media®, Inc.
(800) 842-4197
www.plaidonline.com

Craf-T Products
(507) 235-3996
www.craf-tproducts.com

C-Thru® Ruler Company
(wholesale only)
(800) 243-8419
www.cthruruler.com

DMD Industries, Inc.
(800) 805-9890
www.dmdind.com

Dr. Ph. Martin's®
(800) 843-8293
www.docmartins.com

Ellison® Craft and Design
(800) 253-2238
www.ellison.com

Fiskars, Inc.
(715) 842-2091
www.fiskars.com

Funky Fibers
(928) 21-FUNKY
www.funkyfibers.com

Golden Oak Paper
(509) 325-5456

Halcraft USA, Inc.
(212) 367-1580
www.halcraft.com

K & Company
(888) 244-2083
www.kandcompany.com

Making Memories
(800) 286-5263
www.makingmemories.com

Marvy® Uchida
(800) 541-5877
www.uchida.com

Paper Adventures (wholesale only)
(800) 727-0699
www.paperadventures.com

Paper Garden (wholesale only)
(702) 639-1956
www.mypapergarden.com

Paper Patch® (wholesale only)
(801) 253-3018
www.paperpatch.com

Sailor Corporation—no contact info available

Sakura Hobby Craft
(310) 212-7878
www.sakuracraft.com

Sizzix
(866) 742-4447
www.sizzix.com

Staedtler® Inc.
(800) 927-7723
www.staedtler-usa.com

Un-du® Products, Inc.
(888) 289-8638
www.un-du.com

X-acto by Hunt Corporation
(800) 283-1707
www.hunt-corp.com

For more information on Mrs. Grossman's stickers and sticker art techniques, you are welcome to contact us at Mrs. Grossman's, P.O. Box 4467, Petaluma, CA 94955, (800) 429-4549. Visit our Web site for even more scrapbook project ideas at www.mrsgrossmans.com.

MEMORY MAKERS

Memory Makers Books is the home of *Memory Makers*, the scrapbook magazine dedicated to educating and inspiring scrapbookers. To subscribe, or for more information, call 1-800-366-6465. Visit us on the Internet at www.memorymakersmagazine.com to learn more about our books and magazine products.

Index

For more great scrapbooking ideas see these popular Memory Makers books.

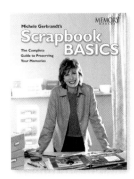